I0410914

NEXT STEPS FOR U.S. FOREIGN POLICY ON SYRIA AND IRAQ

HEARING

BEFORE THE

SUBCOMMITTEE ON
THE MIDDLE EAST AND NORTH AFRICA

OF THE

COMMITTEE ON FOREIGN AFFAIRS
HOUSE OF REPRESENTATIVES

ONE HUNDRED THIRTEENTH CONGRESS

SECOND SESSION

NOVEMBER 19, 2014

Serial No. 113–223

Printed for the use of the Committee on Foreign Affairs

Available via the World Wide Web: http://www.foreignaffairs.house.gov/ or
http://www.gpo.gov/fdsys/

U.S. GOVERNMENT PRINTING OFFICE

91–457PDF   WASHINGTON : 2014

For sale by the Superintendent of Documents, U.S. Government Printing Office
Internet: bookstore.gpo.gov   Phone: toll free (866) 512–1800; DC area (202) 512–1800
Fax: (202) 512–2104   Mail: Stop IDCC, Washington, DC 20402–0001

COMMITTEE ON FOREIGN AFFAIRS

EDWARD R. ROYCE, California, *Chairman*

CHRISTOPHER H. SMITH, New Jersey
ILEANA ROS-LEHTINEN, Florida
DANA ROHRABACHER, California
STEVE CHABOT, Ohio
JOE WILSON, South Carolina
MICHAEL T. McCAUL, Texas
TED POE, Texas
MATT SALMON, Arizona
TOM MARINO, Pennsylvania
JEFF DUNCAN, South Carolina
ADAM KINZINGER, Illinois
MO BROOKS, Alabama
TOM COTTON, Arkansas
PAUL COOK, California
GEORGE HOLDING, North Carolina
RANDY K. WEBER SR., Texas
SCOTT PERRY, Pennsylvania
STEVE STOCKMAN, Texas
RON DeSANTIS, Florida
DOUG COLLINS, Georgia
MARK MEADOWS, North Carolina
TED S. YOHO, Florida
SEAN DUFFY, Wisconsin
CURT CLAWSON, Florida

ELIOT L. ENGEL, New York
ENI F.H. FALEOMAVAEGA, American Samoa
BRAD SHERMAN, California
GREGORY W. MEEKS, New York
ALBIO SIRES, New Jersey
GERALD E. CONNOLLY, Virginia
THEODORE E. DEUTCH, Florida
BRIAN HIGGINS, New York
KAREN BASS, California
WILLIAM KEATING, Massachusetts
DAVID CICILLINE, Rhode Island
ALAN GRAYSON, Florida
JUAN VARGAS, California
BRADLEY S. SCHNEIDER, Illinois
JOSEPH P. KENNEDY III, Massachusetts
AMI BERA, California
ALAN S. LOWENTHAL, California
GRACE MENG, New York
LOIS FRANKEL, Florida
TULSI GABBARD, Hawaii
JOAQUIN CASTRO, Texas

AMY PORTER, *Chief of Staff*   THOMAS SHEEHY, *Staff Director*
JASON STEINBAUM, *Democratic Staff Director*

———

SUBCOMMITTEE ON THE MIDDLE EAST AND NORTH AFRICA

ILEANA ROS-LEHTINEN, Florida, *Chairman*

STEVE CHABOT, Ohio
JOE WILSON, South Carolina
ADAM KINZINGER, Illinois
TOM COTTON, Arkansas
RANDY K. WEBER SR., Texas
RON DeSANTIS, Florida
DOUG COLLINS, Georgia
MARK MEADOWS, North Carolina
TED S. YOHO, Florida
SEAN DUFFY, Wisconsin
CURT CLAWSON, Florida

THEODORE E. DEUTCH, Florida
GERALD E. CONNOLLY, Virginia
BRIAN HIGGINS, New York
DAVID CICILLINE, Rhode Island
ALAN GRAYSON, Florida
JUAN VARGAS, California
BRADLEY S. SCHNEIDER, Illinois
JOSEPH P. KENNEDY III, Massachusetts
GRACE MENG, New York
LOIS FRANKEL, Florida

CONTENTS

NEXT STEPS FOR U.S. FOREIGN POLICY ON SYRIA AND IRAQ

WEDNESDAY, NOVEMBER 19, 2014

House of Representatives,
Subcommittee on the Middle East and North Africa,
Committee on Foreign Affairs,
Washington, DC.

The subcommittee met, pursuant to notice, at 3:25 p.m., in room 2172, Rayburn House Office Building, Hon. Ileana Ros-Lehtinen (chairman of the subcommittee) presiding.

Ms. Ros-Lehtinen. The subcommittee will come to order. Thank you so much. And I am so sorry that we had a slew of votes, but I always say, as a Cuban refugee, that we love getting interrupted by democracy in action. So thank you very much for sticking around.

After recognizing myself and Ranking Member Deutch for 5 minutes each, because they are all coming back from the votes, for our opening statements, I will then recognize other members seeking recognition for 1 minute. We will then hear from our witnesses. And without objection, the witnesses' prepared statements will be made a part of the record, and members may have 5 days to insert statements and questions for the record subject to the length limitation in the rules.

The Chair now recognizes herself for 5 minutes.

One of the first hearings this subcommittee held during this Congress focused on the situation in Syria 2 years into its violent conflict. This will be our 10th hearing dedicated to examining the Syrian conflict, the precarious situation in Iraq, and the rise of ISIL. I wish I could say that we are here today to see how things have gotten better, but as we know, we can't say that.

The common theme we have seen in our previous nine hearings is that the administration has failed to put together a coherent, a consistent, and decisive policies and strategies to address these threats. We have gone from remaining silent when the Syrian opposition first spoke out against Assad in March 2011, before all the foreign fighters and the terrorist groups coopted the anti-Assad campaign, to finally calling on Assad to step down 5 months after his brutal crackdown began, and back to remaining silent again, and allowing Assad to remain in power.

We remain on the sidelines dithering and indecisive until President Obama laid down his now infamous red line on Syrian chemical weapons. As we know, Assad unleashed chemical weapons on

(1)

his people, and that red line was crossed without any repercussions for Assad, damaging our credibility in the region.

We now know Assad did not fully disclose all of his chemical weapons, materials, and stockpiles, and therefore, that threat still remains. Now, after over 3 years of fighting in Syria, President Obama has decided to arm and train Syrian rebels, but not in the fight against Assad, and these rebels are supposed to fight against ISIL, but only in a defensive posture. I believe this strategy is a mistake.

In the immediate aftermath of the fall of Mosul earlier this year, Secretary Kerry said that Mosul's fall took everyone by surprise. Yet 7 months before the fall, then Deputy Assistant Secretary Brett McGurk said, ''ISIL has benefitted from a permissive operating environment due to inherent weaknesses of Iraqi security forces, poor operational tactics, and popular grievances. It has also benefitted from a sanctuary across the porous border in Syria, control of lucrative facilities there, such as oil wells, and regular movement of weapons and fighters between Syria and Iraq.''

He would go on to say that we knew the Iraqis lacked the equipment for the relentless and effective operations against ISIL in Iraq. So how is it the President, the Secretary of State, and others in the administration can say that after Mosul fell that it was a surprise? The President then authorized air strikes in Iraq and eventually in Syria to target ISIL. This may be a case of too little too late, because it is becoming evident that we need a stronger and broader approach.

Our allies in the gulf and the coalition are ready and eager to support us in the battle against ISIL, but they need to see a U.S. that is committed to the fight. They just aren't seeing that now and expect a more comprehensive approach, which includes removing Assad from power, and that means addressing the Iranian issue.

The Maliki government failed because it allowed Iran to exert undue influence over Iraq, which marginalized and angered the Sunni people in that country. Iran's support for Assad has kept that thug in power and has caused the Syrian conflict to continue and escalate, soon entering its fourth year. Our strategy to fight ISIL will not be effective if we don't have a comprehensive strategy that looks at Iraq, Syria, and ISIL linked together.

In Iraq, thanks to the brave fighting from the Kurds and a new Iraqi Government, we have been able to stall the progress of ISIL fighters. Iraqi forces have been able to drive out ISIL fighters from oil refineries seeking to take aim at ISIL's lifeline, its financial support.

This terror group is well financed, and we need to target its source of income as part of our comprehensive approach if we are to succeed. However, more needs to be done. The new Iraqi Government must learn from the mistakes of Maliki and maintain stronger relations with the Kurds. One example can be helping in immediately rearming the Kurds. The Kurds have been fighting on the front lines against ISIL, and they are in real need of more weapons, ammunition, and supplies.

But most importantly, the President needs a strategy that tackles the issues of Iraq, Syria, and ISIL together, because, if not, the

crisis will spill over across the Middle East and pose an even greater threat to U.S. national security interest.

And I am now pleased to yield to—Mr. Kennedy is walking
over—be pleased to yield to members for their opening statements
while we wait for Mr. Deutch. He is coming. So we will start with
Mr. Kennedy.

Mr. KENNEDY. It is a first-time experience for a freshman, thank
you very much, to be first. Madam Chair, I just want to thank you
for hosting a very important hearing.

To the witnesses, thank you for your service. Thank you for being
here yet again to brief this committee. I very much look forward
to hearing what you have to say as we dive into some of the details
and an update from all of you. So thank you very much. I look forward to your testimony.

Ms. ROS-LEHTINEN. Thank you very much, Mr. Kennedy.

And someone who has been in the fight over there, Mr. Cotton
is recognized.

Mr. COTTON. Well, with a late start to the hearing and 6 years
of excessive and long-winded oratory before me in the Senate, I will
cede back my time to the chair so we can hear from the witnesses.

Ms. ROS-LEHTINEN. Thank you very much.

Mr. Higgins of New York is recognized.

Mr. HIGGINS. I would defer to the chair, too, to hear the witnesses.

Ms. ROS-LEHTINEN. Thank you.

Another veteran in our subcommittee we are so proud of, Mr.
DeSantis.

Mr. DESANTIS. Thank you, Madam Chairman.

You know, I was really rattled when a couple of weeks ago The
Wall Street Journal reported that the President wrote a secret letter to Ayatollah Ali Khamenei from Iran seeking to enlist Iran's
support in the fight against ISIS. The idea that the way to defeat
a terrorist group is to align ourselves with the world's leading state
sponsor of terrorism is flatly unacceptable, and I fear that that will
be used as consideration to provide even more concessions to Iran
for their nuclear program. And the result of this policy could be
catastrophic where Iran acquires the bomb and they increase their
sphere of influence throughout the Middle East where you have a
Shi'a crescent from the Afghanistan border to the Mediterranean
Sea.

And so I am glad we are talking about ISIS, it is an important
subject. And I just want to make my position clear: Iran has no
constructive role in the fight against ISIS. They sponsor terrorism.
They view us as the great Satan. They want to destroy Israel. And
the President is way off base if he thinks otherwise. And I yield
back.

Ms. ROS-LEHTINEN. Thank you, sir.

Mr. Schneider of Illinois.

Mr. SCHNEIDER. Thank you, Madam Chair, and thank you to the
witnesses. In the interest of time, I will yield back my time so we
can get to the testimony and hear their ideas for the way forward.

Ms. ROS-LEHTINEN. Thank you, sir.

Dr. Yoho of Florida.

Mr. YOHO. Thank you, Chairman Ros-Lehtinen, for holding this hearing, the 10th of its kind, and secondly, thank you to the witnesses that are coming before us today.

Since 2011, the administration has been unable to adequately address the deteriorating situations in Iraq and Syria that have given rise to ISIL. Since ISIL's rise, many innocent lives have been lost to the brutality, the crucifixions, the decapitation. They are thugs, plain and simple, thugs who have taken advantage of a power vacuum created by an unclear U.S. foreign policy that resembles a broken compass, and it has created uncertainty in the resolve of the United States and the direction for our allies to follow. I look forward to your testimonies, thank you.

Ms. ROS-LEHTINEN. Thank you very much, Dr. Yoho.

And now I am pleased to recognize our witnesses. Thank you for your patience. First we are pleased to welcome the Honorable Robert Ford, who is a 30-year veteran of the State Department. Ambassador Ford has served our country in Bahrain, in Iraq, in Algeria, and most recently in Syria. What have you been doing wrong?

He has also served as the U.S. Ambassador to both Algeria and Syria. He is currently a resident scholar at the Middle East Institute and teaches at Johns Hopkins University.

We welcome you, Ambassador Ford.

We are also pleased to welcome back a good friend of our subcommittee, the Honorable Elliott Abrams, who is a senior fellow for Middle Eastern at the Council of Foreign Relations. Previously he has served as deputy assistant to the President and deputy national security advisor in the administration of President George W. Bush, where he supervised U.S. foreign policy in the Middle East for the White House.

Welcome, Mr. Abrams.

And also returning is our good friend, Dr. Kimberly Kagan. She is the president and founder of the Institute for the Study of War. Previously she taught at the U.S. Military Academy in West Point and has served in Kabul from 2010 to 2012, working for General David Petraeus and General John Allen.

Thank you.

And last but not least, a very good gentleman. We welcome Dr. Steven Heydemann, who serves as the vice president for applied research on conflict and is also a senior advisor on the Middle East at the United States Institute for Peace.

We have got quite a great lineup. Thank you very much. Your written statements will be made a part of the record.

And, Ambassador Ford, we will begin with you.

STATEMENT OF THE HONORABLE ROBERT STEPHEN FORD, SENIOR FELLOW, MIDDLE EAST INSTITUTE (FORMER U.S. AMBASSADOR TO SYRIA)

Mr. FORD. Thank you very much, Madam Chairman and honorable members of the committee. It is really an honor to be with you this afternoon.

I worked in Iraq on the ground for 4½ years between 2003 and 2010, and I worked on Syria for 3 years after that, including just a little over 1 year on the ground in Syria. And especially with respect to Syria, the situation has become really atrocious. Several of

5

you talked about the threat that jihadi elements in Syria and Iraq pose, so I won't go over that, but I think it is important to understand that what this really is, is it is one big conflict stretching from Syria across the border and over to Iraq. It is one conflict. There is a western front and there is an eastern front.

The eastern front in Iraq where Iraqi Government policies alienated not only Sunni Arabs, but also Kurds, created such tensions inside Iraq, this is during the time of former Prime Minister Maliki, such tensions inside Iraq that resistance against the Islamic State was disjointed and quite ineffective.

The good news over the last several months is that on the eastern front in Iraq the advance of the Islamic State has been blunted. Our strikes and the material assistance that we have provided have certainly contributed. And another little bit of good news from the Iraq side is that there is some progress, don't want to overstate it, but there has been some progress resolving political differences between the central government in Baghdad and the Kurdish Regional Government.

That said, again on the eastern front in Iraq, the central government's dependence on armed Shi'a militias is really very alarming. They are using Shi'a militias primarily as their weapon against the Islamic State. Human Rights Watch and Amnesty International last month published very detailed reports, I recommend them to you, about the abuses which these Shi'a militias are committing against Sunni Arab communities where they operate in Iraq. And to be very clear, those abuses are going to prevent us from winning the hearts and minds of Iraq's Sunni Arabs. And without Iraq's Sunni Arabs, no sustainable containment, much less the destruction of the Islamic State in Iraq is going to be possible.

Reining in those militias is going to be hard given the Iranian role in helping them. Thus, going forward, the administration is going to have to be quite tough about what to do with respect to the Shi'a militias and the Iranian influence. I have no doubt that our commitment to a genuinely inclusive political arrangement in Iraq is going to be really tested.

I am going to say a few things about Syria. The situation, as I said, is absolutely terrible. The air strike campaign which we started in September has actually hurt the moderate opposition. It has discredited them on the street because we struck targets belonging to the al-Qaeda-affiliated al-Nusra Front, which had being fighting the Assad regime. I am not arguing that these elements should not have been hit, but at a minimum we should have been explaining to Syrians, both civilians and moderate fighters, what our strategy was and why we were hitting the al-Nusra Front.

In addition, we have directly helped the outside regime by hitting Islamic State targets in eastern Syria that were fighting not Iraqis, these Islamic State units were not fighting the moderate opposition, they were fighting the Assad regime, and our air strikes enabled the Assad regime to break the siege of units surrounded in one of the provincial capitals in eastern Syria. In fact, what we did is we played the role of the Assad air force there. Interestingly, we have provided no close air support to moderate elements near Aleppo that are desperately fighting the Islamic State and also confronting the Assad regime.

So going forward, if it continues like this, there isn't going to be a moderate opposition in northern Syria, and I wonder then who is it exactly that is going to face the Islamic State. The U.N.'s capable envoy Steffan DeMistura is proposing a freeze, sort of a cease-fire, and it is a laudable idea, could allow humanitarian aid to get through. But there have been dozens of efforts to get a cease-fire, and they have almost all failed because there hasn't been an enforcement mechanism.

Nor will a freeze, a cease-fire, in Aleppo or Damascus address the jihadi problem. And so going forward, I think the administration is going to have to decide if it wants boots on the ground to confront jihadis or not, and if it does want boots on the ground, whose boots are they going to be? There aren't any easy choices, but the perfect answer cannot be the enemy of the good at this point.

Secondly, the administration is going to have to decide if it wants a political process or not, and if it does want a political process it is going to have to figure out how to get to one. The current path is not going to get to a political process and instead it is going to get to an environment where it is going to be even harder to fight jihadis.

So with that rather grim assessment, thank you very much, and I look forward to your questions.

[The prepared statement of Mr. Ford follows:]

Mr. Chairman, Ranking Member Engel,

It is an honor to come before you today to discuss events in Iraq and Syria.

I spent 4 1/2 years working in Iraq on three assignments between 2003 and 2010 and I worked on Syria in Damascus and then from Washington for three years between 2011 and 2014.

When I was on the ground in Iraq, and later in Syria, we never saw a group as potent as the Islamic State. My colleague, former ambassador Ryan Crocker, calls the Islamic State "al-Qaida version 6.0." Its thousands of fighters, many of them veterans, its administrative capacity, its financial resources and its recruiting savvy all present a big challenge first to regional stability but also to our national security.

The Islamic State stretches in the West from the outskirts of Aleppo, what was Syria's second-largest city, across the Syrian and Iraqi deserts and over that World War I era Syria-Iraq border to the outskirts of Baghdad with Mosul, Iraq's second largest city, firmly under the Islamic State's control. This is now a single conflict across Syria and Iraq.

On the western front, the Syrian side, there is little to be hopeful about.

On the eastern front, the situation in Iraq is very difficult, but not as desperate as it was during the peak of the fighting there in 2005 until 2008. Indeed, there are hints of military progress on the ground, as well as some progress on the political front. The administration's strategy that links our military support to political inclusiveness in Baghdad may yet yield sustainable progress against the Islamic State.

Most important, the military situation in Iraq has shifted against the Islamic State. Iraqi security and Shia militia forces have slowly forced the Islamic State's fighters to leave parts of Diyala province northeast of Baghdad, as well as from towns near southern Baghdad like Jarf as-Sukhr and Muademiyah - what we used to call the "triangle of death." Iraqi security and Shia militia forces in recent days pushed Islamic State forces out of Baiji and its important refinery north of Baghdad.

It's not 1945 but it could well be late 1942.

The administration's rushing assistance to Kurdish fighters - Peshmerga - as well as its help to steady remaining elements of the Iraqi Army have helped hugely, as have American airstrikes.

There are some hopeful signs on the political side too:

The central government in Baghdad and the Kurdish regional government for the first time agreed on a formula to start negotiations over their differences about the budget and the oil sector.

This is important to the Kurds: they have heavy military expenses as well as costs from its hosting over 200,000 Syrian refugees as well as some 850,000 Iraqi internally displaced persons (many from Mosul when the Islamic State captured the city last June). Their civil servants have had salary disruptions.

And this preliminary agreement is important to Baghdad - it shows the world that Iraq can solve tough political problems and demonstrates that the new government under Prime Minister Abadi is politically agile.

There is still far to go to reconcile the Kurdish Regional Government and the government in Baghdad. In particular, they must come to an agreement about how to manage oilfield development and exports. This will be especially harder given the Iraqi government's budget deficit due to lower oil exports and export prices.

And the Americans and the international coalition need to be careful as well. Merely arming the Kurds without also pushing for a sustainable political agreement between the Kurds and Baghdad will set up future battles over oilfields and land between the central government and the Kurds. We need to urge compromises on the two sides.

Finance Minister Hoshyar Zibari is close to the Kurdish Regional Government and the Oil Minister, Adil Abdel Mehdi, is from the Shia political coalition but in my firsthand experience relates well to the Kurdish political leadership. These two men are very capable, they are men of good will and if empowered to reach a conclusive deal that would settle the big problems between the central government and the Kurdish Regional Government. I am sure the administration is encouraging them forward.

It is vital for the stability of Iraq that a durable Kurdish-Baghdad deal be reached.

And it is vital to finding a sustainable, durable solution to the Islamic State problem in Iraq that Iraqi Sunni Arabs agree to join the fight against the Islamic State.

Here too there are some hopeful signs.

Above all, the Islamic State's own atrocious brutality is helping. Its massacres of Sunni Arab tribes' members in areas under its control have alienated many Sunni Arabs. Local councils in Anbar, Mosul and Salah ad-Din have called for volunteers from their Sunni Arab communities to fight the Islamic State. They claim that they will fight if given the material support. They also claim that this material support has been very slow to arrive.

Prime Minister al-Abadi is a very capable politician; his personality is very different from that of his predecessor. He has shown some sensitivity to the Sunni Arabs, and he also began to address the deep corruption problems in the Iraqi army by firing a couple dozen generals two weeks ago.

The Prime Minister has not, and cannot, however, fix all the sectarian problems that stress relations between Sunni and Shia Arabs in Iraq, however.

Many Shia, as well as Kurdish,, leaders are reluctant to give the Sunni Arab fighters arms. They fear the Sunni Arabs might one day use those same weapons against the Shia and the Kurds. The National Guard legislation has not yet received approval in Baghdad. Yet, without help from Baghdad, Sunni Arab population won't mobilize against the Islamic State. So again, we will have to be engaged not just with military advisors but also at a political level.

Moreover, the government in Baghdad depends on Shia militias, some of which are on our terrorism list, to push back against the Islamic State. Amnesty International and Human Rights Watch recently provided detailed reports about serious abuses committed by these militias against Sunni Arab civilians during the fighting. NPR earlier this week did a similar story about abuses against Sunni civilians at the hands of Kurdish Peshmerga. If forced to choose between the Islamic State or Shia or Kurdish militias, Sunni Arab communities will choose the Islamic State for safety. Thus, the Baghdad and Kurdish regional governments must tame those militias if we are to gain lasting Sunni Arab support against the Islamic State in Iraq. That will be hard - the Iranians and their friends inside the Iraqi government are promoting those Shia militias.

These difficulties pale in comparison to the challenges in Syria, however.

The plan to launch airstrikes now against the Islamic State and later train vetted fighters from the Syrian opposition to confront the Islamic State is not succeeding. The Islamic State advance stalled at the town of Kobani but elsewhere, such as in central Syria, the Islamic State's fighters are still advancing slowly.

Moreover, we have pounded Islamic State targets in Deir Zour where they confronted surrounded military units of the Asad regime. Those attacks enabled the regime to reopen previously closed supply lines and shift military assets, especially air assets, against moderate armed opposition fighters around Aleppo. In a sense, we have been Asad's air force in eastern Syria.

We pound Islamic State targets at Kobani where they are fighting a Kurdish group affiliated with the terrorist PKK organization. We are the Kurds' air force even though this is angering the Turks whose help against the Islamic State is vital if we are ultimately to destroy the group.

We have never attacked the Islamic State close to Aleppo where it confronts moderate Syrian fighters. So the moderates, fighting a two-front war against Asad and the Islamic State, received no direct relief from any of our attacks.

Instead, our air operations in northwestern Syria directly harmed the moderate armed groups. Our strikes against elements of the al-Qaida affiliated Nusra Front led the Nusra Front to suspect the moderates we've helped are, in fact, an American-backed fifth column against jihadis. Thus, Nusra two weeks ago launched a pre-emptive attack against moderate elements in northwestern Syria. Nusra largely routed them.

We didn't warn the moderate fighters about our strategy and what it could encompass, so they were surprised and unprepared for the air attacks and what Nusra Front response. Oddly, we don't discuss strategy with them at all, they tell us.

Squeezed between the Asad regime and the jihadis, the moderate armed groups in northern Syria will not survive if this American/Coalition approach continues. Their morale problems are worse. They are more isolated politically as they get blamed for being American agents when other Syrians fighting the Asad regime get bombed by American aircraft. In a few months I doubt there will be a moderate opposition in the North.

Instead, there will be only jihadis from Nusra and the Islamic State against the Asad regime and Kurds allied with it. And I cannot see how that will help us contain, much less roll back, the Islamic State.

The UN's very capable envoy Steffan DeMistura has proposed a "freeze" in hostilities in Aleppo in the North since he thinks that both the moderate opposition and the regime now understand they face a common enemy in the Islamic State.

DeMistura's proposal would, if accepted by all sides, allow for humanitarian aid to reach Aleppo, a very laudable goal. The suffering of the Syrian people in cities like Aleppo is unimaginable.

There have been many local ceasefire attempts in the past but nearly all failed because there was no enforcement mechanism. Monitors don't suffice, as we saw with the ineffective UN observer mission in 2012.

An enforcement mechanism can't work without international backing. Regional states and international states providing material support to both sides in the conflict must agree about the utility of such ceasefires. And these countries must use their influence to ensure the warring sides abide by ceasefire terms. We've never had this yet; there is no international consensus about what to do about Syria.

Moreover, local ceasefires in a places like Aleppo won't deal with the jihadi problem. The Nusra Front and the Islamic State, both of which have forces near Aleppo, would not accept a ceasefire even if Asad does. Moreover, it is extremely unlikely that what remains of the moderate opposition in the North would join with Asad forces against Nusra or the Islamic State. After all the brutality, it is a fantasy to hope for such an alliance. Already one of the groups we have worked with, the Hazm Movement, has agreed to a truce with the Nusra Front so that they can both concentrate against the Asad regime in Aleppo.

And if the fighting in Aleppo did diminish, very likely the Asad regime would shift scarce military forces elsewhere, thus escalating fighting in the places like the Damascus suburbs and the South where the moderate opposition is still fighting.

Realistically, therefore, unless we dramatically change our tactics, the moderates will not be able to contain the jihadis of Nusra and the Islamic State even if we do some day train five or ten thousand fighters.

For its part, the Asad regime lacks the manpower to move into eastern Syria. Even if it could scrounge up the manpower, Syrian regime forces only advance with the help of Iranian and Hizballah forces. The presence of Iranian and Hizballah forces in eastern Syria would aggravate suspicions among Sunni Arabs in western Iraq that Iranian and surrogate forces are surrounding them from east and west. Those fears would impede bringing Iraqi Sunni Arabs on board against the Islamic State on the eastern front.

Thus, the Islamic State will enjoy a secure base in eastern and central Syria for the foreseeable future. The strategic depth the Islamic State will enjoy in Syria will in turn hinder efforts to destroy its forces in Iraq as well.

———

Ms. Ros-Lehtinen. I have a bill on the floor, which is wonderful news, but Mr. DeSantis is a very able substitute for me. Thank you.

Mr. DeSantis [presiding]. While we are changing chairman, Mr. Deutch, ranking member of the subcommittee, has arrived.

So did you want to make your opening statement?

I recognize the gentleman from Florida.

Mr. Deutch. Thank you, Mr. Chairman, and my apologies to the witnesses.

Thanks to our esteemed panel for appearing here today. I would like to recognize Ambassador Ford for your years of service and acknowledge all of the foreign service officers, military personal, and humanitarian workers who have committed themselves to addressing the crisis in Syria and in Iraq.

Mr. Chairman, I believe this is now the 10th hearing related to either Iraq or Syria that this subcommitteehas held this Congress. President Obama first said that Bashar al-Assad must go in August 2011. We were told that it would be just a matter of months. Yet the Assad regime held one, aided in large part by an Iranian assistance, and the regime continued its murderous rampage for another 3 years.

Over 200,000 people have died in this conflict, and while the international community may have succeeded in ridding Assad of his chemical weapons arsenal, he continues to use other brutal tactics, like barrel bombs, and has literally resorted to starving people to death by cutting off access to aid.

As we struggled to determine who in the Syrian opposition we could work with, some in the gulf were busy funding extremist elements that had gained popular support simply because they were the best organized and on and off the battlefield. As horrified as we were at the tactics of groups like Jabhat al-Nusra, a group denounced for its violence by al-Qaeda, something worse was growing. The rise of ISIS has thrown Syria and Iraq into chaos, igniting thousands of years of sectarian conflicts, straining the fatigued Syrian opposition's resources as they now battle both Assad and ISIS, and destabilizing Iraq to levels of violence not seen since before 2006.

ISIS grabbed ahold of large swaths of territory in Syria, marched into Iraq, rendering the border between these two countries obsolete, declaring an Islamic caliphate. When ISIS forces overran Mosul and began targeting religious minorities, the United States made the decision to intervene. I applaud the administration for working to then secure a broad coalition that includes over 60 international partners acting in various capacities to combat this threat, but after months of air strikes, it is time to look at what we have accomplished and how we intend to proceed in our effort to, as the President said, degrade and destroy ISIS.

Air strikes halted ISIS' march toward Erbil, which would have put significant American interests and personnel at risk. Air strikes helped to rescue the Yazidi population from Mt. Sinjar and secure the Mosul dam. Air strikes have prevented the takeover of Kobani on the Turkish border. But air strikes won't end the conflict; neither will American boots on the ground. The people of Iraq and Syria, with training and equipment from the U.S. and our partners, are the only ones who can end this conflict.

To that end, we must continue to support the Peshmerga and the Syrian Kurds, the Iraqi security forces, and the moderate Syrian opposition, while simultaneously encouraging political processes in both Iraq and Syria. In Iraq, this government must work to unite with the Sunni communities against ISIS. This government cannot repeat the mistakes of the past. An inclusive dialogue that brings Sunni, Shiite, and Kurds to the table is the best and, frankly, only way to stabilize Iraq against ISIS forces.

Regional partners must play a leading role in encouraging Iraq's new leaders to work in concert with Sunni tribes in Anbar. Regional partners must also work with the U.S. to support the Iraqi and Syrian Kurds, and I am pleased that there has been progress made in allowing access to weapons and aid, as well as a significant step by the Turkish Government to allow the Peshmerga to pass through its territory. Turkey, a NATO ally, must play a vital role in international efforts to combat this threat, and I hope that Vice President Biden's visit to Turkey will increase this cooperation.

I understand these are complicated relationship. The Washington Post recently addressed these complexities explaining that the Peoples' Democratic Party, or PYD, to which the Kurds fighting in Kobani belong, is affiliated with the Kurdistan Workers' Party, or PKK, which Turkey and the U.S. Have designated a terrorist organization. The PKK in turn has ties to the Assad regime, the Iraqi Kurds have close relations with Turkey and the U.S. and are affiliated with a different Syrian Kurdish faction, the Kurdish National Council, which backs the Syrian opposition and is at odds with the PYD over who should control the Kurdish regions of Syria.

This only further emphasizes why the international community must work to unite opposition factions in both the fight against ISIS and the fight against Assad. I welcomed the announcement last week that the administration will reassess its strategy in Syria and Iraq, because this unfortunate reality is that as long as the Syrian conflict rages on, ISIS will continue its deadly assault in both Syria and in Iraq. It will continue its recruiting of foreign fighters. It will continue to build up proxy groups in the region. And with so much international focus on ISIS, Assad has continued his assault on the Syrian people with near impunity. It is no wonder that the Assad regime is continuing to purchase ISIS' oil, generating millions per day in funding for its terrorist activities. As long as ISIS continues its atrocities, Assad will attempt to convince the world that he is now the lesser of two evils.

Mr. Chairman, there are no easy answers here, and I commend the administration for the progress it has made. I urge our partners in the region to assist us in accelerating the training and equipping of Syrian opposition. I commend the allies in the region who have stepped up to this fight. But we, in conjunction with our partners, must have a long-term strategy, and I look to our witnesses today to provide us with some guidance. I thank you, and I yield back.

Mr. DeSantis. The gentleman yields back. And we will continue with the witness statements. I will go to Elliott Abrams.

You are recognized for 5 minutes.

STATEMENT OF THE HONORABLE ELLIOTT ABRAMS, SENIOR FELLOW FOR MIDDLE EASTERN STUDIES, COUNCIL ON FOREIGN RELATIONS

Mr. ABRAMS. Thank you, Mr. Chairman.

I appreciate the opportunity to be here today. I remember testifying here and in the Armed Services Committee a couple of years ago and saying there are 100,000 people killed and a couple of million refugees. Of course now about 200,000 dead, perhaps 7 million refugees, which are completely changing the politics, the economies, the demography of Jordan, Lebanon and Kurdistan.

So you have asked in the name of this hearing what next, what steps. We all share the goal of defeating ISIS, the Islamic State, or destroying it, as the President once said. But I don't think we have a strategy in place today that can achieve that goal, primarily because we do not really have a sensible Syria strategy.

And our strategy in Iraq is comprehensible but unlikely to succeed, in part because, as the Ambassador said, there is one military theater here, there is an eastern front and a western front, but Syria and Iraq now are one theater because ISIS obliterated the border. So if we don't have a Syria policy, we don't really have an Iraq policy.

To start with Iraq, the question really is, who is going to fight ISIS? And our answer seems to be a combination of the Iraqi Army, the Sunni tribes, and the Kurdish Peshmerga. They will fight, and they will defeat ISIS with our help. That strategy is not working yet, and one reason is that we have been so slow to commit the forces we are likely to need, a few hundred people, then 1,500 people, now another 1,500 people.

Now, if we need exactly 3,000 advisors, I am glad we have the right number, but I wonder if it is the right number, and if not, if it is not, let's commit the number we need now rather than in a drawn-out series of announcements that assure we will always have too few forces in theater.

Moreover, though we have watched the Peshmerga having great difficulty dealing with ISIS, We continue to deny those forces military aid they seek and they need. That is not going to work. If our goal is to limit Iranian influence and defeat ISIS, strengthening the Peshmerga is the logical step, and we should take it.

Last week a key Kurdish official, Mansour Barzani from the National Security Council, said this in an interview: ''We have told the international forces there is a continuous need to support the Peshmerga with sophisticated arms in order to repel the ISIS enemies and defeat them as quickly as possible. The arms the Peshmerga have today are the old arms that came from the former Iraqi Army. As for the military assistance that reached the Kurdish region,'' I am still quoting Barzani, ''this comprises medium weaponry and ammunition. The only heavy weaponry that we have yet received is some antitank missiles supplied by Germany.''

That is not going to work. ''The Western states that have pledged military assistance to the Peshmerga have yet to meet their promises,'' he also said. It is not going to work.

As to the Sunnis, we seem to be waiting for Baghdad to arm them. A couple of weeks ago General Dempsey said the precondition for arming them is that the Government of Iraq has to be willing to arm the Sunni tribes. We are going to be waiting a long time, I think, before we see the Government of Iraq do that, and we are running out of time

In Syria, I agree with the Ambassador. We don't seem to have any answer at all to the question who is going to fight ISIS unless the answer is the Assad regime and Iran and Hezbollah. We have been very, very slow to help turn the rebels into an effective fighting force. It is very sad, it is tragic that the advice to help them from Secretary Clinton and CIA Director, later Secretary of Defense Panetta, and Secretary Kerry was rejected by the President.

So now we seem to be falling into a kind of alliance with Iran and the Assad regime. And for all the reasons the Ambassador said, it is not going to work. It was really the Assad regime's brutality that created ISIS. A Syria policy that relies on Iran and Hezbollah and the Assad regime cannot succeed.

I would just quote Ambassador Fred Hof, who was, with Ambassador Ford, one of the key Obama administration officials handling Syria policy until he resigned. He noted that the White House press statement introducing their November 7 fact sheet on Iraq strategy doesn't mention Syria, and as Hof says, "the Assad regime cannot, short of its voluntary departure, be part of a legitimate governance answer in Syria."

The next steps, I think, arm the Peshmerga, arm the Sunni tribes in Iraq, arm the Syrian rebel groups. To defeat ISIS, we must change the situation in Syria. The Assad regime is a jihadi manufacturing machine. We face a situation today, as the Ambassador said, where we occupy the Syrian air space, but Assad's air force can, with impunity, carry out any crime against humanity, any air strike against civilians, and we do nothing about it.

If we continue to target and weaken ISIS without stepping up our help to the rebels, we are clearing the field for the Assad regime. There is no magic formula we can have here. As Fred Hof put it, "A Goldilocks approach of trying to recruit and build a force just good enough to beat ISIL but not quite good enough to beat the regime simply won't work."

Thanks again for inviting me to testify. This is a complicated situation, as all of you have said. Every path ahead is fraught with difficulty. But this is the 10th hearing, and I just want to thank you for the committee's diligence in looking at Iraq and Syria over the past 3 years. Thank you.

Mr. DeSantis. Thank you.

[The prepared statement of Mr. Abrams follows:]

COUNCIL on
FOREIGN
RELATIONS

November 19, 2014

Next Steps for U.S. Foreign Policy on Syria and Iraq

Prepared statement by
Elliott Abrams
Senior Fellow for Middle Eastern Studies
Council on Foreign Relations

Before the
Subcommittee on the Middle East and North Africa
Committee on Foreign Affairs
United States House of Representatives
2nd Session, 113th Congress

Hearing on "Next Steps for U.S. Foreign Policy on Syria and Iraq"

Madam Chairman and Members of the Subcommittee:

Thank you for this opportunity to testify today.

Sixteen months ago I testified before the House Armed Services Committee on the situation in Syria, and in that testimony noted that 100,000 Syrians had already been killed. As you meet today, the number of those killed is now over 200,000. And it now is estimated that more than 7 million Syrians are refugees or displaced persons. These refugee flows have completely changed the demography, the economies, and the politics of Jordan and Lebanon—and all the numbers continue to grow.

And as I noted in that 2013 testimony, the continuation of this conflict is itself a threat to U.S. interests and allies. There are perhaps a million and a half Syrian refugees in Lebanon and the same number in Jordan.

Neither country has the capacity to deal with them. The Kingdom of Jordan is one of our key allies in the Middle East and stability there should be a prime concern of ours. As the conflict continues and more and more jihadis arrive in Syria, we must also wonder about their role in Lebanon and along the Syrian-Israeli border. Their growing presence in the area is another serious threat.

The purpose of this hearing is not to cry over spilt milk but to ask what we do next. In my view, we should have three goals: to alleviate the humanitarian situation and help friendly countries deal with the refugee crisis; to prevent an Iranian victory in Syria that would be a great blow to American interests; and to strike devastating blows at the Islamic State.

All of us share that goal of defeating the Islamic State, or to use the tougher term the President once used, destroying it. But I do not think we have a strategy in place today that can achieve that goal.

Why not? Because we have no sensible Syria strategy. And our strategy in Iraq is comprehensible but unlikely to succeed—in part because there is now one Syria/Iraq military theater, ISIS having obliterated the border. If we have no Syria policy, we have no realistic ISIS policy.

Let me begin with Iraq. The question is who will fight ISIS. Our answer appears to be that a combination of the Iraqi army, Sunni tribes, and the Kurdish Pesh Merga will fight and defeat ISIS—with our help. As of today, that strategy is not yet working. One reason is that we have been slow to commit the forces we are likely to need, sending a few hundred, then a total of 1500, then 1500 more. If we need exactly 3,000 advisers and no more, I am glad we will have them; but I wonder if that is really the right number. If it is not, let's commit to the number we need now rather than in a drawn-out series of announcements that assure we will always have too few forces in theater. Moreover, though we have watched the Pesh Merga have great difficulty dealing with ISIS, we continue to deny those forces the military aid they seek. That will surely not work. If our goal is to limit Iranian influence and defeat ISIS, strengthening the Pesh Merga seems like a logical step. We should take it.

Last week a key Kurdish official, Mansour Barzani of the Kurdish national security council, said this in an interview about military aid:

> "We have told the international forces that there is a continuous need to supply the Peshmerga forces with sophisticated arms in order to repel the [ISIS] enemies and defeat them as quickly as possible. The arms that the Peshmerga have today are the old arms that came from the former Iraqi army," he told Asharq Al-Awsat.

> "As for the military assistance that reached the Kurdish region, this comprises medium weaponry and ammunition. The only heavy weaponry that we have yet received is some anti-tank missiles

supplied by Germany. So the Kurdish region has yet to receive any other weapons that will allow us to change the balance of power on the ground in favor of the Peshmerga," he added.

Barzani particularly criticized Iraqi military assistance to Kurdish forces, which he said was practically non-existent.

"Baghdad should have provided far more [military assistance] than it has. Baghdad should have provided the Peshmerga forces with sophisticated weaponry . . .But we have seen nothing like this," he said.

He added that the western states who have pledged military assistance to the Peshmerga have yet to meet these promises, calling on the international community to do more as ISIS "is not waiting for us to be armed to attack us." [http://www.aawsat.net/2014/11/article55338237]

As to the Sunni tribes, we appear to be waiting for the government in Baghdad to arm them. A couple of weeks ago Gen. Dempsey was quoted as saying, after a massacre of Sunnis in Anbar province, that "we need to expand the train, advise and assist mission into ... Anbar province. But the precondition for that is that the government of Iraq is willing to arm the tribes." [http://english.alarabiya.net/en/News/middle-east/2014/10/31/Iraq-s-top-Shiite-calls-on-Baghdad-to-help-Sunni-tribes-after-killings.html] We may wait a long time to see that happen, and meanwhile ISIS can gain additional victories.

We should step back for a moment and see how our overall policies may appear from the Sunni perspective. In Syria, which I will come back to shortly, we've watched 200,000 mostly Sunnis killed, and watched continuing criminal attacks against the Sunni civilian population using artillery and so-called barrel bombs, and done almost nothing. We backed away from our own red line when chemical warfare was used against Sunni civilians there. It appears that we and other Western governments will be arming the Kurds before we will be arming the Sunnis in Iraq. We bombed near Kobani in Syria to save Kurds. We acted to save the Yazidis in Iraq, but not the Sunnis there or in Syria. We may be about to conclude our negotiation with Iran over nuclear weapons. The President just sent a letter to the Ayatollah Khamenei in which he "sought to assuage Iran's concerns about the future of its close ally, President Bashar al-Assad of Syria," according to *The Wall Street Journal. The Journal* says the letter "states that the U.S.'s military operations inside Syria aren't targeted at Mr. Assad or his security forces." What are Sunnis to make of that, when Assad continues to kill Sunni civilians every single day? [http://online.wsj.com/articles/obama-wrote-secret-letter-to-irans-khamenei-about-fighting-islamic-state-1415295291]

We all want to defeat and destroy ISIS. But recruiting for ISIS continues, on the basis that Sunnis are threatened and must be defended. To young Sunni males from Europe, the Middle East, Asia, and even the United States, this will continue to be an attractive argument unless we can defeat ISIS ideologically as well as militarily. Today, our policies can too easily be depicted by ISIS propaganda as indifferent or hostile to Sunnis and indeed as seeking an accommodation with Shia forces and with Iran.

It is in that context that I turn to Syria. In Syria, we have no answer at all to the question who will fight ISIS—unless our answer is the Assad regime and its Iranian and Hezbollah supporters. Our plans for helping turn the rebels into a more effective fighting force have been extremely slow to develop. As you know, that step was urged several years ago by Secretary Clinton and CIA Director and later Secretary of Defense Panetta, and then over a year ago by Secretary Kerry. Unfortunately their good advice was rejected by the President, so we are way behind now and the programs are unfolding very slowly-- to be kind. If you detect a note of urgency in how the administration is handling this question, I do not.

Instead we appear to be falling into a sort of alliance with Iran and with the Assad regime. But it is the vicious brutality and the war crimes of that regime against the 75% of Syrians who are Sunnis that largely created ISIS, which then grew with great speed and moved also into Iraq.

In my view a Syria policy that relies on Iran, Hezbollah, and the Assad regime cannot succeed. And if we have no realistic Syria strategy, we have no realistic Iraq strategy, because ISIS will just move a bit west into Syria to rest and recruit and rearm.

Let me cite here the words of Ambassador Fred Hof, now at the Atlantic Council but from 2009 to 2012 a key Obama administration official handling Syria policy. Like former ambassador Robert Ford, the other key official handling Syria policy, Hof resigned when he could no longer really defend the policy. Here's part of what he wrote last week:

> At Andrews Joint Base on March 14, 2014 President Barack Obama told visiting uniformed defense chiefs that a key aspect of destroying the Islamic State in Iraq and al-Sham (ISIS, also known as ISIL and the Islamic State) would be the promotion of moderate, legitimate governance inside Syria; governance that would ultimately be extended to all Syrians. On November 7, 2014 the White House published its strategy for "degrading and ultimately defeating ISIL:" nine lines of effort to that end. Which of the nine addressed the all-important element of moderate, legitimate governance in Syria? None. What is going on here? [....]
>
> It is understandable that the United States and the coalition it has assembled have as the near-term top military priority the slowing and reversal of ISIS military momentum in Iraq. Yet something else seems to be unfolding: the virtual erasure of Syria from the equation, and less than a month after President Obama assured coalition defense chiefs that he fully understood the centrality of good governance in Syria to the destruction of ISIS. Indeed, the White House press statement introducing the November 7 fact sheet on strategy avoids mentioning Syria altogether. [....]
>
> The Assad regime cannot—short of its voluntary departure—be part of the legitimate governance answer in Syria. Its application of war crimes and crimes against humanity—all administered with a strong sectarian flavor—made central and eastern Syria fertile ground for ISIS and its foreign fighters. It works in tandem with ISIS to terrorize Syrians and erase the nationalist opposition.

If the fact sheet of November 7, 2014 truly reflects the administration's strategy to combat ISIS, it is missing a major piece: Syria. Until that piece is covered in a way that addresses reality in Syria, the overall strategy itself will inevitably fall short of the goal of "degrading and ultimately defeating ISIS." [November 12, 2014, "Countering ISIS: Obama Administration Strategy" by Frederic C. Hof, http://www.atlanticcouncil.org/blogs/menasource/countering-isis-obama-administration-strategy]

I agree fully with this analysis.

I would add that such a policy will be seen by everyone in the region as a defeat of the United States by Iran. On one side, Iran, Hezbollah, and Russia support Assad; on the other, the United States, EU, and our Sunni Arab friends from the Gulf say he must go. Does it matter who wins? Yes—because around the world but especially in the Middle East allies and enemies will judge the power, influence, and willpower of the United States and our friends in no small part by the outcome of this conflict.

Should the Assad regime be replaced by a Sunni regime oriented toward Syria's Sunni neighbors, this will be a huge defeat for Russia, Iran, and Hezbollah. Involvement in Syria is already arousing discontent among Lebanon's populace, including Shia who wonder why their sons are dying for Bashar al-Assad, and a defeat in Syria will undermine Hezbollah inside Lebanon. Its power has been rising there for decades; now, a turning point might be reached and it might start declining. Given Hezbollah's global reach as a terrorist group, that's very much in our interest.

Similarly and even more importantly, the unceasing rise of Iranian power in the region would be seen to have been stopped if the Assad regime falls. Iran's influence has been viewed as growing steadily— partly due to the demise of a hostile Sunni regime in Iraq (at America's hands) and to growing Iranian influence there; partly to Iran's perceived role in places like Bahrain, Saudi Arabia's Eastern Province, and most recently in Yemen; partly to Iran's steadily advancing nuclear program; and partly to the sense that America, the overwhelming power in the Middle East since World War II, lacked the desire or ability to stop Iran. If we defeat Iran in Syria, all this is changed and what King Abdullah of Jordan once called the "Shia crescent" stops being cemented.

Remember that Iran's only Arab ally is Syria, which also provides it with Mediterranean ports and a land bridge to Hezbollah in Lebanon—and through Hezbollah, Iran gets a border with Israel. This all changes if Assad falls.

Conversely, what happens if we decide the game in Syria is not worth the fight, and the war goes on until Assad more or less crushes the rebellion? What happens if we make common cause with Iran and Assad? Many more refugees, threatening stability in Jordan and Lebanon. Iranian ascendancy, strengthening

Hezbollah inside Lebanon and Iran throughout the Middle East. An emboldened Iran, seeing a lack of American desire to confront it, is logically more likely to become more aggressive in Bahrain, the home of our Fifth Fleet, in Saudi Arabia's heavily Shia Eastern Province, in Yemen, and in its own nuclear program.

So what should our next steps be? As I have mentioned, I believe we should be doing far more to equip the Pesh Merga, the Sunni tribes in Iraq, and the Syrian rebel groups. As to the latter, I do not trust the self-fulfilling prophecies that say they cannot fight when they have in fact been fighting, for years now, without our help and with enormous losses of men.

To defeat ISIS we must change the situation in Syria. The Assad regime is a jihadi manufacturing machine. I also believe we should consider again a strike at Assad's air assets as part of our activities in Syria. Air power continues to be an important weapon for Assad against the rebels. We need to make it clear to Assad that those assets may not be used to terrorize the populace and murder thousands more civilians in more war crimes and crimes against humanity. We face today the situation where we occupy Syrian air space but Assad's air force can carry out any crime against humanity and any air strike against civilians or rebel forces that it wishes. As we know, Assad has often used his military far more enthusiastically against the rebels and against civilians than against the jihadis. We need to tell him the rules are going to change. He can use those air assets against ISIS — or he will lose them.

We must realize that if we continue to target and weaken ISIS without stepping up our help to the rebel forces, what we are doing is clearing the field for the Assad regime. It should not be acceptable to us to create a situation where regime forces move in after ISIS forces move back due to U.S. bombing. So it is time to get serious about building a Syrian rebel force that can some day take power in Syria because it represents and is based in the 75% of the population that is Sunni. Fred Hof put it best in an interview last month:

> A Goldilocks approach of trying to recruit and build a force just good enough to beat ISIL but not quite good enough to the beat the regime simply won't work."
> [http://www.businessinsider.com/obama-isis-syria-rebels-assad-2014-10#ixzz3J3PJD0PI]

Thank you again for inviting me to testify. We all realize that the situation in Iraq and Syria is extremely complex and that every path ahead is fraught with difficulty. But we also recognize that American interests are at stake here, so I thank this Subcommittee for delving deeply into the challenges we face and the alternative policies from which we must choose.

Mr. DESANTIS. We will now go to Dr. Kagan for 5 minutes.

STATEMENT OF KIMBERLY KAGAN, PH.D., FOUNDER AND PRESIDENT, INSTITUTE FOR THE STUDY OF WAR

Ms. KAGAN. Thank you very, very much to you and to all of the members.

We face a real threat emanating from the Middle East, and it is not contained simply to the Middle East. We are looking at an incredibly dangerous enemy in the Islamic State and its rival living in Syria, the al-Qaeda affiliate Jabhat al-Nusra, the al-Nusra Front. And we are looking at two terrorist groups right now that are competing with one another for stature and global posture in order to claim the legitimacy and the leadership of the global jihadist movement. There is a huge amount at stake in Iraq and Syria, and it is not contained within their borders.

I have rendered to you in my written testimony my assessment agreeing very much with the members of the committee, with Ambassador Ford, with Ambassador Abrams it's fact the American strategy in Iraq and Syria is flawed. Fatally, that its focus simply on degrading and destroying ISIS at the expense of looking at the regional and global conflicts that compromise the security of the United States and in which the United States has incredible interests is damaging the way we can approach future years and future generations as an American power.

In point of fact, our strategy being pursued in isolation against the Islamic State, ignoring Assad, ignoring the rather extraordinary and complex dynamics within the global jihadist movement itself is really creating conditions for a fight that will last not just the coming years, but the coming generations. So we have a problem, and we need to solve it, and those solutions will not be simple, they will not be facile, and they will not be easy.

We must recognize that our current strategy is not only driving the moderate opposition into a degree of marginalization such that it will no longer exist and flourish when we think that we really must rely on it to succeed in Syria. We are also actually creating conditions in which the competition between Jabhat al-Nusra and the Islamic State are going to characterize the future fight for Syria.

We also, I think, are really underestimating the way in which the temporary solutions that the Iraqi Government and security forces are undertaking against ISIS right now inside of Iraq will actually drive the conflict over the long term. As Ambassador Ford noted, the Iraqi security forces are essentially not the same Iraqi security forces that we left behind in 2011. They are now plussed up with command and control elements, as well as fighting forces that come from Iranian-backed proxy groups that had, in fact, been fighting inside of Syria. And so what we are actually watching on the ground in the temporary halting of ISIS through deprivation, through denial of terrain in Bayji, and through denial of terrain in Jurf al-Sakhar, a very important stronghold south of Baghdad, is actually really creating the conditions in which an Iranian-backed Iraqi Government, based mostly around the security forces that are run by Iran, can actually establish a frontline that runs through the Shi'a areas of Iraq and pushes the Islamic State into a wedge between Iraq and Syria. These conditions, frankly, are allowing the Islamic State to consolidate its gains inside of Iraq because of the sheer fear of the Sunni population at facing something that is not a legitimate security force but really an arm of the Iranian Government.

We need to refocus our policy. If we want there to be moderate opposition to Assad and if we want the Sunni tribes actually to rise up against al-Qaeda, we need to provide them with asymmetric capabilities on the battlefield so that they can achieve those objectives. Namely, they need close air support, they need command and control from us, and they need the ability to change the game so that they can survive the dual and triple threats that they are facing.

Thank you very much.

Mr. DeSantis. Thank you.

[The prepared statement of Ms. Kagan follows:]

Next Steps for U.S. Foreign Policy on Syria and Iraq

House Foreign Affairs Committee
Subcommittee on Middle East and North Africa
November 19, 2014

Statement of
Dr. Kimberly Kagan
President and Founder
The Institute for the Study of War

Institute for the Study of War
1400 16TH STREET NW | SUITE 515 | WASHINGTON, DC 20036   WWW.UNDERSTANDINGWAR.ORG   202.293.5550

American strategy in Iraq and Syria continues to suffer from a fatal flaw. President Obama explicitly ordered that it focus only on "degrading" and "destroying" the Islamic State to the exclusion of any other American national security interests and regardless of the likelihood of the long-term success of any such effort undertaken in isolation. As a result, the strategy has achieved some limited successes against the Islamic State, but those isolated successes are coming at the expense of other important American security concerns. The current approach, in particular, has strengthened the position of Iran, its armed forces, and its proxies in Iraq, and has allowed al Qaeda affiliate Jabhat al Nusra to expand its control and influence in Syria. These trends are very likely to continue if the U.S continues to pursue the present strategy.

Chairman of the Joint Chiefs of Staff, General Martin Dempsey, recently said that the battle against the Islamic State is beginning to turn, but that the campaign to defeat it would take several years. He also said that he might have to recommend the deployment of additional American forces and their use in combat alongside Iraqi troops to retake the city of Mosul. I agree with his assessments and I continue to believe that U.S. forces will, indeed, be needed to clear Mosul. The current change of momentum provides a good opportunity to consider the likely outcome of the present effort in Iraq, its potential stability, and the degree to which it coheres with American national security interests. It is also an important moment to remember that there is no parallel campaign in Syria, where the situation continues to worsen as Jabhat al Nusra gains territory, the Islamic State retains the lands it had taken, Bashar al Assad continues to murder his own people, and such moderate opposition as there is receives little meaningful support.

U.S. strategy in Iraq today relies on a combination of Iraqi Security Forces (which are fundamentally different from what we left behind in 2011), Popular Mobilization Units (hastily-trained anti-ISIS volunteers, largely from Shi'a areas), Iranian-controlled Shi'a militias, a limited number of Sunni tribal volunteers, and some Iranian Revolutionary Guards Corps (IRGC) and Qods Force advisers (including Major General Qassem Soleimani, commander of the Qods Force, himself).

American strategy complements Iranian goals, perhaps inadvertently. Iran is pursuing a strategy in Iraq that is analagous to the one it has been pursuing in Syria. It will create in Iraq a security structure in which anti-American Iranian-backed militia commanders operate side-by-side and overtly with Iraqi Security Forces with a degree of interdependence that will make them inseparable. Such a force can never be representative of Iraq as a whole, and will never be accepted over the long term by any of Iraq's minority populations. It will also be antithetical to American interests in the long term, while remaining a vector for Iranian control and influence. The outcome of this approach will be unstable and will entrench Iran in Iraq at the expense of America and our allies.

The Obama Administration still has not articulated any strategy in Syria. U.S. efforts there appear confined to a limited number of airstrikes, carefully restricted to hit only Islamic State or Khorasan Group targets. On the rare occasions when Jabhat al Nusra fighters have been hit, the White House has moved rapidly to deny that it was targeting them. The U.S. has taken no measures to weaken the Assad regime militarily. Assad therefore continues to fly combat aircraft and helicopters and to use them to conduct barrel-bombing attacks and other atrocities against his own people. Assad has nevertheless lost ground to the Islamic State, and is struggling to maintain a presence in eastern Syria. He has also lost ground in Dera'a and Quneitra south of Damascus to Jabhat al Nusra and other rebel forces. The forces that the U.S. has nominally been backing have suffered losses at the hands of the Islamic State, Jabhat al Nusra, and the regime.

The current trajectory in Syria, therefore, will likely lead to a situation in which Jabhat al Nusra and some of its Salafist allies control significant areas south of Damascus and in the Idlib countryside; the Islamic State retains control of much of the Euphrates River Valley; the regime continues to fight for Damascus, controls the M5 highway to just past Hama, and controls the coast; and the moderate opposition remains marginal and incapable of shaping the battlefield in any material way.

President Obama has misdefined our mission in Iraq and Syria by attempting to deal with one problem in isolation from its context and from the many other challenges facing the U.S. We have seen this movie before. The Bush Administration also misdefined the problem in Iraq before 2007, believing that an inclusive political process combined with assistance to the nascent Iraqi Security Forces would solve the problem. Both administrations then fell into the trap of focusing on measures of progress that were relevant only within the narrowly-constrained view of the situation they had decided to confine themselves to. Thus the Bush administration kept briefing the acres of territory turned over to Iraqi security leads and highlighting Iraqi security operations that were actually sectarian cleansing undertakings that made the underlying problem worse. The Obama administration is likewise focused on reporting progress only in limited areas--strikes conducted against Islamic State positions, however trivial, and limited tactical gains made by the highly-sectarian and Iranian-dominated security forces on the ground.

We must raise our gaze from the tactics of fighting the Islamic State. We need a strategy not only to disrupt and defeat the Islamic State, but also to reduce Iranian influence in the region rather than expanding it, to develop inclusive Iraqi security forces rather than sectarian units intertwined with militias and the Qods Force, and to bring the Sunni tribes in Iraq once more to the negotiating table to hammer out a revised political deal with the Shi'a dominated government in Baghdad rather than helping that government try to simply crush them.

And we need a strategy in Syria. It must not hand Syria's Sunnis over to either the Islamic State or Jabhat al Nusra. It must not leave Assad in power. It must expel Lebanese Hezbollah from Syria. And it must find and build up a moderate opposition among Syria's Sunni, 'Alawites, and Kurds who will be able one day to form a new, inclusive government acceptable to the Syrian people. Any strategy that aims at lesser goals is a recipe for permanent sectarian and regional proxy war that will provide an excellent safe-haven for al Qaeda-affiliated groups and Iranian terrorist allies in Syria, and will ultimately undermine any stability that might be achieved in Iraq as well.

Dr. Kimberly E. Kagan is the founder and president of the Institute for the Study of War. She is a military historian who has taught at the U.S. Military Academy at West Point, Yale, Georgetown, and American University, and is the author of a number of books and numerous essays. Most recently, she is the co-author (with Frederick Kagan and Jessica D. Lewis) of *A Strategy to Defeat the Islamic State*. ISW has tracked and predicted the rise of ISIS since late 2011 and that research may be found in *"Predicting the Rise of the Islamic State"* at www.UnderstandingWar.org.

Dr. Kagan previously conducted regular battlefield circulations of Iraq between May 2007 and April 2010 while Gen. Petraeus and Gen. Raymond T. Odierno served as the MNF-I Commanding General. She participated formally on the Joint Campaign Plan Assessment Team for Multi-National Force-Iraq in October 2008 and October 2009, and as part of the Civilian Advisory Team for the CENTCOM strategic review in January 2009.

In addition, she served in Kabul for 17 months from 2010 to 2012 working for commanders of the International Security Assistance Force, Gen. David H. Petraeus and subsequently Gen. John Allen. Dr. Kagan also served as a member of Gen. Stanley McChrystal's strategic assessment team, comprised of civilian experts, during his campaign review in June and July 2009. Admiral Mike Mullen, as Chairman of the Joint Chiefs of Staff, recognized Dr. Kagan for this deployment as a volunteer with the Distinguished Public Service Award, the highest honor the Chairman can present to civilians who do not work for the Department of Defense.

She is the author of *The Eye of Command* (2006) and *The Surge: A Military History* (2009), and editor of *The Imperial Moment* (2010). Dr. Kagan has published numerous essays in outlets such as the *Wall Street Journal*, *New York Times*, *Washington Post*, *Los Angeles Times*, *Weekly Standard*, and *Foreign Policy*. She co-produced "The Surge: The Whole Story," an hour-long oral history and documentary film on the campaign in Iraq from 2007 to 2008.

Dr. Kagan held an Olin Postdoctoral Fellowship in Military History at Yale International Security Studies in 2004 to 2005 and was a National Security Fellow at Harvard's Olin Institute for Strategic Studies in 2002 to 2003. She received her B.A. in Classical Civilization and her Ph.D. in History from Yale University.

Mr. DeSantis. We will now go to Dr. Heydemann for 5 minutes.

STATEMENT OF STEVEN HEYDEMANN, PH.D., VICE PRESIDENT OF APPLIED RESEARCH ON CONFLICT, UNITED STATES IN-STITUTE OF PEACE

Mr. Heydemann. Thank you, Mr. DeSantis, and my thanks as well to Chairman Ros-Lehtinen and Ranking Member Deutch, and other members of the subcommittee for convening this hearing. I have to begin my comments by noting that the views I express today are solely my own and do not represent the U.S. Institute of Peace, which does not take positions on policy issues.

As the chairman noted in her opening remarks and as a number of my colleagues here today have also stressed, more than 3 years since Syria collapsed into civil war the U.S. still lacks a coherent, integrated strategy either to achieve a political solution to the Syrian conflict or to degrade and destroy ISIS. A reassessment of Syria policy by the White House is called for and would be a welcome acknowledgment of the need for such a strategy.

Given conditions on the ground, the relevant questions that a review must address concern not only what can be done to degrade and destroy ISIS, but how U.S. policy can help consolidate effective governance by moderate opposition actors, retrieve the possibility of a negotiated settlement of the Syrian conflict, and help Syrians preserve a path between extremism and dictatorship.

An effective response to these questions will require moving beyond the policy of containment that has defined U.S. policy for the past 3 years. It will also require moving beyond a policy of local cease-fires. Instead, the starting points for an integrated strategy need to include a clear understanding that efforts to degrade and destroy ISIS either in Syria or in Iraq will not be successful unless they are accompanied by broader U.S. engagement anchored in a framework for moving Syria toward a political transition based on the Geneva Protocol of June 2012.

The proposed train-and-equip program is an important piece of such a strategy. This should not only be placed on a fast track, as Secretary Hagel has promised will be the case, it also should be given a mission that extends beyond containing or rolling back ISIS to include operations targeting the Assad regime forces.

To succeed, however, the train-and-equip mission will also require more extensive support from the U.S. and its regional partners through the establishment of a no-fly zone over northern Syria and a buffer zone inside Syria's border with Turkey. These should be supported by the active participation of broad regional and international coalition.

To ensure that appropriate command and control is in place as fighters become operational, it will be necessary to link U.S.-trained forces to effective elements within existing Syrian opposition institutions. Without such a framework, the U.S. train-and-equip mission will be precarious, the effectiveness of U.S.-trained forces against ISIS diminished, and the possibilities for a political solution to the Syrian conflict remote. With them, U.S.-trained opposition forces will be able to operate from Syrian territory with oversight provided by Syrian military and political leadership. In addition, effective elements among the opposition's leadership will be able to move inside the country where they will be better positioned to support local councils and strengthen governance across opposition-held areas of the country.

Perhaps most important, however, the combination of a protected buffer zone and a better trained and better equipped armed opposition has the potential to affect the strategic calculus of the Assad regime, revive negotiations, and advance efforts to achieve a political transition that includes acceptable elements from the regime and the opposition and preserves what remains of the institutions of the Syrian state.

The Assad regime has been relentless in its pursuit of a military victory, secure in the support it receives from Russia, Iran, and Hezbollah. The regime is persuaded that international assistance from the opposition for the opposition will remain too limited to affect conditions on the ground. The integrated strategy outlined in my written testimony offers opportunities to more effectively challenge the Assad regime, degrade ISIS, strengthen alternatives to extremism and dictatorship, and create meaningful incentives for both the regime and the opposition to negotiate a political end to the Syrian conflict.

Thank you, and I look forward to your questions.

Mr. DESANTIS. Thank you.

[The prepared statement of Mr. Heydemann follows:]

UNITED STATES INSTITUTE OF PEACE

· · ·

An independent institution established by Congress to strengthen the nation's capacity
to promote peaceful resolution of international conflicts

"Next Steps for U.S. Foreign Policy on Syria and Iraq"

Testimony before the House Committee on Foreign Affairs
Subcommittee on Middle East and North Africa
U.S. House of Representatives

Steven Heydemann
United States Institute of Peace

November 19, 2014

Good afternoon and thank you to the House Foreign Affairs Subcommittee on Middle East and North Africa Chairman Ros-Lehtinen, Ranking Member Deutch, and other members of the subcommittee for this opportunity to testify before you on U.S. policy toward Syria and Iraq. The views I express today are solely my own and do not represent those of the United States Institute of Peace, which does not take policy positions.

Toward an Integrated Syria Strategy: Summary and Recommendations

More than three years since Syria collapsed into civil war, and facing the most widespread violence in the modern history of the Middle East, the US still lacks a coherent, effective strategy to degrade and destroy ISIS, or achieve a political solution to the Syrian conflict. These goals cannot be achieved through policies that view ISIS and the Syrian conflict as separate. To paraphrase a great statesman, the US cannot fight ISIS as if there is no Syrian conflict, and pursue a political solution in Syria as if there is no ISIS. It must do both, and must put in place an integrated strategy for Syria that acknowledges the connections between the two. The recently announced review of Syria policy by the White House is a welcome recognition of the need for such a strategy. To be effective, the review should be guided by the following considerations.

• An integrated Syria strategy will require the US to expand its engagement with the Syrian opposition, improve prospects for a change in the balance of power on the ground, and help create the conditions necessary for a negotiated end to the conflict.

• Such an approach will require US support for a no-fly zone over northern Syria and a protected buffer zone along Syria's border with Turkey.

• The proposed train and equip program for the Syrian opposition should be accelerated and its mission expanded to encompass both confronting ISIS and challenging the Assad regime.

• To ensure oversight and accountability for opposition forces trained with US support, and to strengthen Syrian alternatives to extremism and dictatorship, both the train and equip mission and the governance of a buffer zone should be linked to effective elements within existing Syrian opposition institutions.

From Bad to Worse: Deteriorating Conditions on the Ground

The options available to the US in Syria were poor in 2011, 2012, and 2013. They are worse today. US airpower has checked the expansion of ISIS but has not yet materially weakened ISIS' position in either Iraq or Syria. Despite air strikes and support from Iraqi Kurdish forces and Free Syrian Army fighters, ISIS still controls significant ground in the border town of Kobani. Nor have airstrikes eroded ISIS' appeal to new recruits, who continue to flock to its banner in record numbers. The

US air campaign has permitted the Assad regime to expand its attacks on moderate opposition forces in Syria and tighten its siege of Aleppo, which may soon fall to the regime. It has further eroded views of the US among Syrian Sunnis and moderates, who, understandably, ask why the US has not used its air power to protect them from the violence of the Assad regime. US airstrikes have also provoked a backlash from Jabhat al-Nusra, al-Qaeda's affiliate in Syria, which has attacked and defeated two of the moderate battalions in northern Syria that were viewed by the US as likely partners in its train and equip program. The moderate armed opposition, which has been steadily losing ground to extremist forces, is now a marginal presence in opposition-held areas.

These battlefield gains by Jabhat al-Nusra in northeast Syria and the possible, perhaps likely, fall of Aleppo to the Assad regime highlight the limits of a stand-alone train and equip program. Given the setbacks experienced by the moderate opposition, it is increasingly unclear how recruitment and vetting will proceed, or what the command and control structure for US-trained units will be. It is not yet clear to whom US-trained forces will report. Civilian authorities to which they will be accountable have not been identified. How the areas in which these forces operate will be governed has not been established. Nor have necessary connections been made between the train and equip program and the broader aim of US policy: to assist in creating conditions on the ground that will be conducive to re-launching negotiations and achieving a political settlement of the Syrian conflict.

Reassessing US Policy in Syria

The current review of US policy offers an opportunity to establish an effective, integrated political strategy for Syria. Given conditions on the ground, the relevant questions that the Administration's review must address concern not only what can be done to degrade and destroy ISIS, but how US policy can help consolidate effective governance by moderate opposition actors in areas from which ISIS is cleared, retrieve the possibility of a negotiated settlement of the Syrian conflict, and assist Syrians in preserving a path between extremism and dictatorship—initially at the local level and eventually at the national level.

Developments on the ground in Syria, combined with the urgent threat posed by ISIS, amplify the costs of inaction for the US and for our partners in the region. These developments make it especially important that the policy review announced by the White House not become a missed opportunity. To avoid this will require moving beyond the policy of containment that has defined the US approach to Syria for the past three years. It will also require more than local ceasefires. Instead, the starting points for an effective US strategy need to include a clear understanding of the Assad regime's role in fueling the rise of ISIS, and the recognition that US efforts to degrade and destroy ISIS will not be successful unless they are accompanied by a political framework that will move Syria toward a negotiated political transition based on the Geneva Protocol of June 2012.

The proposed train and equip program is an important piece of such a strategy. This should be placed on a fast track for implementation but also given a mission that extends beyond containing or rolling back ISIS to include operations targeting Assad regime forces. For the train and equip program to succeed, moreover, it must be accompanied by more extensive support from the US and its regional partners, including Turkey. It must be enabled through the establishment of a no-fly zone over northern Syria along the Turkish border, as well as a buffer zone inside northern Syria. Both a no-fly zone and a buffer zone should be supported by the active participation of a broad regional and international coalition. To ensure that appropriate accountability mechanisms and command and control structures are in place as fighters become operational it will also be necessary to link US-trained forces to effective elements within existing Syrian opposition institutions.

A no-fly zone and buffer zone will require a significant expansion of US engagement in Syria. Without them, however, the train and equip mission will be precarious, the effectiveness of US-trained forces against ISIS diminished, and the possibilities for a political solution to the Syrian conflict remote. With them, US-trained opposition forces will be able to operate from Syrian territory, with oversight provided by the opposition's military and political leadership. Effective elements among the opposition's political leadership and the interim Syrian government will be able to move inside the country. They will have the opportunity, once and for all, to earn the legitimacy they currently lack and persuade Syrians that their future is not limited to extremism or dictatorship. They will also be better positioned to support local councils and strengthen governance across opposition-held areas of the country. In addition, a protected buffer zone may offer Syrian civilians safe harbor from the violence of both the regime and jihadist groups.

Most important, the combination of a protected buffer zone and a better trained and better equipped armed opposition has the potential to affect the strategic calculus of the Assad regime, revive negotiations, and achieve a political transition that includes acceptable elements from the regime and the opposition and preserves institutions of the Syrian state. A protected buffer zone and well-trained opposition forces have the potential to upend the foundations of the Assad regime's strategy, which rest on its conviction that the US and its partners are unwilling to engage on a scale that will affect the outcome of the conflict or threaten the regime's future.

The Assad regime has been relentless in its pursuit of a military victory; secure in the support it receives from Russia, Iran, and Hezbollah, and persuaded that international assistance for the opposition will remain too limited to affect conditions on the ground. The integrated political strategy recommended here will challenge the core assumptions of the regime's strategy, even as they provide the means to degrade ISIS, strengthen alternatives to extremism and dictatorship, and create meaningful incentives for both the regime and the opposition to negotiate a political end to the Syrian conflict.

Beyond Local Ceasefires: Retrieving a Geneva Process

Support for a strategy that includes top-down efforts to affect the strategic calculus of the Assad regime as a condition for re-launching negotiations has faded over the past year. The failure of Geneva II talks in January 2014, regime advances, and the rise of ISIS and other jihadist groups have dimmed interest in such an approach. The train and equip program, for example, has been presented as a response to the growing threat from ISIS. The White House has declined to characterize it in terms of its broader Syria policy, or as a counterweight to the Assad regime. More recently, proposals for local ceasefires have emerged as an alternative to an integrated political strategy. UN Special Envoy Staffan di Mistura has proposed a freeze for Aleppo. His intent is to bring relief to civilians who have endured enormous suffering and establish a model for bottom-up peacebuilding that might then spread to other settings. The Center for Humanitarian Dialogue in Geneva, in a plan yet to be made fully public, advocates a policy of local ceasefires on similar grounds.

Local ceasefires are a potentially positive step and warrant consideration. Measures that hold promise of an end to violence for communities that have endured years of devastating conflict should be pursued. Yet ceasefires are not an alternative to an integrated political strategy. They cannot resolve the deep differences between the Assad regime and its opponents that have sustained Syria's conflict for more than three years. They have not been endorsed by any of the Syrian or regional parties to the conflict, either as a solution for Aleppo or as a general policy. Previous cases of local ceasefires have a mixed track-record, at best. And a strategy that rests on local ceasefires risks providing cover for a regime-imposed settlement that would expand support for extremist groups among Syrians opposed to the regime and undermine prospects for a broader political solution.

To prevent such an outcome, local ceasefires should be pursued in combination with an integrated Syria strategy designed to degrade and roll back ISIS, support the opposition in its efforts to change the balance of power on the ground, establish a no-fly zone and protected buffer zone, and help to create the conditions necessary for meaningful negotiations between the Assad regime and the Syrian opposition. Under such conditions the Geneva Protocol of June 2012, which remains the only framework for negotiation endorsed by the US, Russia, and other key stakeholder governments, can still provide a useful framework for a negotiated political transition that will end Syria's devastating conflict and permit Syrians to begin the difficult and painful process of post-conflict recovery.

Thank you. I am happy to take your questions.

The views expressed in this testimony are those of the author and not the U.S. Institute of Peace, which does not take policy positions.

Mr. DeSantis. The Chair will recognize himself for 5 minutes. Let me start. I think that, and I think the witnesses enumerated this pretty well, obviously we have the Iraqi forces and we have had mixed results with them and they have had their problems. You have the Syrian opposition, which has some very unsavory elements, and there is obviously a range in their capability. But the one group that I think most of us here in the committee and in the Congress recognize are pretty strongly pro-American are the Kurdish Peshmerga. And, Ambassador Abrams, I concur with your recommendation.

What we are hearing, though, the frustration is we claim we are going to send them these weapons and they have got to get everything through Baghdad. We asked Secretary Kerry when he was here, look, we need to get them the weapons, we can't be going through this. And he said, well, that is on you guys, we are just following the law, we are not allowed to send weapons directly. So is that your understanding? And, I mean, don't you think it would be better for us to just send the stuff directly to them so we can expedite this?

Mr. Abrams. I think it would be better. That way we would know it is getting through. We know now that it is not getting through and that they are fighting with basically rifles and machine guns, nothing better than that, no helicopters, for example, which would be so useful to them. As to the legal aspect of this, I would bow to Ambassador Ford, who no doubt have to handle this part.

Mr. DeSantis. Ambassador, do we need to act in Congress? I mean, Secretary Kerry, I believe, said his hands were tied and he said, hey, that is on you guys, you guys need to change the law. That is interesting. That line of reasoning doesn't seem to apply to immigration. But nevertheless, go ahead.

Mr. Ford. I can't speak to what American law might be applicable, Congressman DeSantis. I can only say that on the Iraq side, the Iraqi constitution, which Kurds ratified as well back in 2005, says that the central government is responsible for defense. And so I think that is one of the reasons the United States has gone through that. There should be a way to negotiate protocol, however, between the Kurds and the central government in Baghdad to expedite things. I mean, frankly, Iraq is living in extraordinary times, and we would expect their political leaders to rise to the occasion.

Mr. DeSantis. Now, you had mentioned the primary defense of Baghdad is really these Shiite militia groups. And I know you have spent a lot of time in Iraq. I was in Iraq 2007 and 2008, and during that time U.S. forces were sustaining a lot of casualties from Iranian-backed Shiite militia groups, EFP attacks, very deadly. Are these basically the same groups as those groups that were attacking U.S. servicemembers?

Mr. Ford. They are indeed. They include Asa-ib Ahl al-Haq, which was responsible for numerous attacks against American soldiers. During your time there, Congressman, you might remember the attack in Hilla that killed five U.S. service men. That is Asa-ib Ahl al-Haq. Kata-ib Hezbollah, which is another one that we confronted, and the Badr Corps, which although I am not aware that they ever attacked American service men, they did kidnap me in 2003, so they have a special place in my heart.

And in all of these instances, Congressman, the Iranian Revolutionary Guard Corps, Quds Force, is providing a great deal of material assistance, command and control. It is amazing how they don't hide this, the commander, General Soleimani, is regularly photographed on the front lines.

Mr. DeSANTIS. That was going to be my next question, and I appreciate that.

Dr. Kagan, and I acknowledge and I mentioned in my opening statement the President wrote a letter to the Ayatollah in Iran. The Wall Street Journal reported that was to show that there is some common interest to fight ISIS with Iran and the United States. I made my feelings, no, I don't think we have common interests. I think that that would make the situation worse. Do you agree that thinking that Iran would be an ally against terrorism would be a bad policy?

Ms. KAGAN. The Iranians are enemies of the United States and have based their regime on an ideology of opposition to America. They do not share our interests and we do not share theirs. So although we may have a minor interest that in narrow circumstances is similar, namely that neither of us likes the Islamic State and both see it as a danger, we do not have the same end states in mind for Iraq, for Syria, for the region, or for the world.

Mr. DeSANTIS. Thank you for that. And, yeah, the thing is we will sometimes hear, well, Iran, they are Shi'a, they oppose Sunni terrorism, and that is not even really true. I do know that they are butting heads with ISIS. But Iran, they funded al-Qaeda operations, they funded of course Hamas. They are one of Hamas's biggest backer, which is a Sunni terrorist group. So Iran, I think, does not have a constructive role in this, and I think that would be really dangerous to go in that direction.

My time has expired, and I will recognize the ranking member, Mr. Deutch, for 5 minutes.

Mr. DEUTCH. Thank you, Mr. Chairman.

Dr. Heydemann, what does a political solution look like for Syria? Does it only focus on Assad? How does ISIS' control over these large swaths of land fit into that strategy. And is there a circumstance—I guess I would throw this open to the panel—is there a circumstance in which the coalition would actually act against Assad or would the United States then lose regional support if we took that approach?

Mr. HEYDEMANN. Thank you. Thank you, Congressman.

One of the reasons that I focus on the Geneva Protocol as a starting point, as a framework for a transition, is because it remains the only framework which has the agreement of the United States, Russia, and a number of other critical stakeholders in this conflict, but also because it sets out a process for determining what a negotiated transition would look like that I believe offers the best possibility for achieving some form of power sharing, an outcome in which it seems very difficult to imagine that the existing leadership of the Assad regime, including President Assad himself, would play a role, but one that I believe holds out some promise for addressing some of the deep and intractable conflicts that sustain the civil war.

38

So the first step, it seems to me, in defining what a political settlement would look like would be to create a negotiating context that would permit the parties to the conflict to move forward in achieving the goals established by the Geneva Protocol, which include creating an interim governing body on the basis of mutual consent of both the regime and the opposition, which would exercise full executive authority, and which could initiate the next steps in a political process that would achieve that broader political solution.

So I continue to see the Geneva Protocol as a useful tool in moving toward a political solution of the conflict.

Mr. DEUTCH. I had said earlier that as we look at this and as we look back, it was the expectation that the Assad government, the regime was going to fall, it was only a matter of when. We heard that not just from our administration, but from leaders in the region. That has not happened.

Ambassador Ford, what should we be saying about our expectations for Assad? Is it possible to wage the battle we are waging now against ISIS without making clear what our ultimate intentions are with respect to Assad and how we are going to accomplish them?

Ambassador Abrams, you, as well.

Mr. FORD. I don't see how it is going to be possible to contain, much less roll back the Islamic State on the western side of this conflict in Syria as long as Bashar al-Assad is running Syria in a way where people can't see an end to it.

It would be great to get to a political negotiation such as Dr. Heydemann was talking about. We tried that in Geneva, and, frankly, we got nowhere. And the opposition in Geneva, I have to mention this, Congressman Deutch, put a very reasonable proposal on the table in the negotiating opening. The U.N. was very pleased with it. The Assad regime completely refused to discuss it. And so, in order to get to a political process, there is just going to have to be more pressure on the Assad regime.

Now, in the 9 months since Geneva the regime has suffered very heavy casualties, and there is more unhappiness among supporters of the Assad regime than there was at the start of 2014. It is very noticeable. There are demonstrations. There are a lot of complaints. The regime has responded with arrests.

So if there is a way to reach out to elements of that regime, to its supporters, and say, look, it doesn't have to be a choice between Assad and jihadi crazies for Syria, there is a third way, then I can imagine moving forward along the lines of Dr. Heydemann's. But in order to do that, you got to have a little more pressure on the regime, too, and we got to get the Russians and the Iranians on board. They also pay attention to the situation on the ground. I go back to what I said, more pressure on the ground.

Mr. DEUTCH. Ambassador Abrams.

Mr. ABRAMS. Well, I agree with that. I think you are not going to be able to achieve that at a negotiating table a result that is independent of the actual facts on the ground. The facts on the ground are what we need to change first. This is a 75 percent Sunni country. It is impossible to think of a role for Assad after he has spent 3 years slaughtering Sunnis.

Mr. DEUTCH. Thank you.

Mr. DESANTIS. The gentleman's time has expired.

The Chair now recognizes my friend from Florida, Ted Yoho, for 5 minutes.

Mr. YOHO. Thank you, Mr. Chairman.

Thank you, panel, for being here. And what I am looking from you, I have got 5 minutes, is a new dynamic, I mean, it won't serve us to go back other than to remember how we got here, to where we go from this point because I have heard all you guys, and I think you guys are very adroit at what you say, I think your experience speaks highly for itself, but it is where we go from here and the policies that you can give us information on how we can bring up legislation to move this situation forward without American boots on the ground.

As you well know, we have had 1.2 million people in Afghanistan and Iraq that are coming back. It is estimated that 600,000 to 800,000 of our troops are going to have some form of PTSD. This is not a road I am willing to go down, but yet this needs to come to an end. Because what I see is an amorphous region with no leader, with no stable government, and we are fighting an ideological member unit, ISIS, that has no country, they have no defined leader, per se, as a normal government would that we would traditionally fight, yet they are the best armed terrorist organization that the world has ever seen. And the best armed, and it scares me to think that the arms they are using are the arms we had in Iraq.

And so, I would like to hear real quickly from each of you. And, Ambassador Abrams, you laid out fairly well what I was looking for.

So, Ambassador Ford, if we could start with you. Legislation that you would say if you would do this, this would help bring stability to that area.

Mr. FORD. There is no easy way to get stability back to that area. I want to be very clear.

Mr. YOHO. We have to have a starting point, though, and if it is arming the Kurds here, so be it.

Mr. FORD. Here are three things that I think the Congress could usefully do. Number one, move forward on an authorization to use military force. It sends a very good message to the Russians. It sends a really good message to the Iranians. And, frankly, it makes Bashar al-Assad nervous. We are not going to be able to get to the political discussion that Dr. Heydemann was talking about, the negotiation, if Bashar al-Assad doesn't feel nervous.

So a solid vote in favor of an authorization to use military force would be very helpful. It sends the right signals.

Second thing, I believe you have coming up again a reauthorization for the use of American funding to train elements, vetted elements of the moderate Syrian opposition. This job is becoming harder because of things that we have done over the last 2 months. That said, that said, it needs to be approved again because it is taking a long time to stand up, but it isn't going to get any easier in 4 or 5 or 6 months. They need to keep moving it forward. I would like them to go faster, but as I said, you can't have the perfect be the enemy of the good.

Third thing, insist, demand that there be accountability among the Iraqi security forces and these Shi'a militia in return for receiving American assistance. We cannot have a situation where the Shi'a militia, Dr. Kagan explained it as well, where they are literally driving the Sunnis into the arms of the Islamic State. We will not win on the eastern front if we do not have those Iraqi Sunnis on board.

Mr. YOHO. All right. I am going to skip over you, Ambassador Abrams, and go to Dr. Kagan.

Ms. KAGAN. I agree with all of Ambassador Ford's recommendations, and in addition I would say that there are two more things that Congress can do to show our strength, not necessarily to use our force. One is that you need to take on sequester and ensure that we have the defense of the United States and the ability to project power in a way that our allies and our enemies can recognize not only now, but over time, and ensure that we have the greatest military in the world still to come.

And secondly, I do encourage you to consider the needs of our intelligence services. And although those intelligence services are under strain both from the pressures that have resulted from the Snowden leaks and also from sequestration, we have a global jihadist threat that is coming to the west, and you need to resource our Intelligence Community such that they have the wherewithal to identify such threats well ahead of time and inform the executive about how it should act.

Mr. YOHO. And, unfortunately, I am out of time.

Dr. Heydemann, if I could get your recommendations and build upon those other ones, I would greatly appreciate it, and we will make sure we institute those.

Mr. HEYDEMANN. Very quickly, two very quick points.

I think it is entirely plausible to use a conversation about authorization and appropriation of a train-and-equip program to remove the artificial restriction on that program as focused solely on ISIS and not on changing conflict dynamics on the ground more broadly and expanding the program.

Second, as I mentioned in my comments, the regime is fully persuaded of the lack of will of the U.S. to engage more deeply, and it seems to me that, as Ambassador Ford said, an authorization for the use of military force that explicitly included the possibility of a no-fly zone and buffer zone would send an extraordinarily powerful signal to the Assad regime.

Mr. YOHO. Thank you, sir.

I yield back, and I apologize to the members for going over. Thank you.

Mr. DESANTIS. Gentleman's time has expired.

And the Chair now recognizes the gentleman from New York, Mr. Higgins, for 5 minutes.

Mr. HIGGINS. Thank you, Mr. Chairman.

I just want to try to provide some context to a situation that I think is sometimes presented as black and white, and there is a lot of gray area. And it is particularly true in Syria where you have the Free Syrian Army, which is made up of some 1,500 militias, which are very organic. They are sectarian. They are mostly, at least, the most effective seemingly Islamic extremists and al-Qaeda affiliates. And we often talk about funding and arming the moderate component of that element, which really makes up a very, very small percentage of the larger group.

And I am also looking at America spent $25 billion building up an Iraqi Army that consists of 283,000 fighters, active; another 528,000 reserves. We talked about in Kurdistan the Peshmerga, which have demonstrated to be reliable allies to the United States. Kurdistan is pretty successful within the context of the Middle East. It is pluralistic. Minority rights are respected. They have been again proven very, very effective.

The last estimates I saw of ISIS in terms of their numbers was from the Central Intelligence Agency, and there were 41,000 estimated ISIS fighters. And it seems to me if you have you an Iraqi Army of well over 280,000, you have got the Peshmerga between 250,000 and 350,000, it begs the question, why is it that we are not more effective in degrading and destroying ISIS immediately? And I think it comes back to the issue that we kind of gloss over, and that is the political issue. And Nouri al-Maliki and his successor have not proven to be inclusive in Iraq.

So the first test of this $25 billion Army that we helped create in Iraq, they ran. They ran. There are political problems now between Iraq and Kurdistan which keeps Iraq from allowing an effective supply of the Peshmerga up in northern Iraq.

So I think the conclusion is that when there is no political center in Iraq or in Syria, there are only sides. And I think we are sometimes led to believe that there is a good side and a bad side. Well, there is often—or there is—a bad side and arguably even a worse side in both of those places, and unless and until you have some kind of recognition of minority rights and inclusion of various groups there, you are never going to have a political situation that is stable which would allow for those countries to evolve.

So what is it that we can do for them that essentially they are responsible for exclusively to create a level of stability that would allow us to fight back effectively or assist them in fighting back effectively against groups like ISIS?

Sorry. A long way to get to a question, but go ahead.

Mr. FORD. Two things come immediately to mind, Congressman Higgins. The first is there are terrible problems of corruption in the Iraqi Army, developed even before Nouri al-Maliki. It was back even in 2005. The very first defense minister in the new Iraqi interim government stole over $1 billion. You mentioned $25 billion. There is $1 billion right there; $1.2 billion, according to the inspector general's office. So there was a problem of leadership and there was a problem of corruption, and I think we absolutely have to hold them more accountable.

That often means that we say we can't work with you on this issue until you fix these seven, eight, nine issues over there. It means, frankly, understanding that if they won't fix themselves, in some cases, there is nothing we can do, and we have to be honest about that.

Second thing, which I should have mentioned with Congressman Yoho's question, in order to do these things, to insist on accountability, we have to step up our own discussions, probably very blunt discussions behind closed doors, but that requires that we be able to get out and about. And we have a large diplomatic team in Iraq. We have a large diplomatic team in places like Turkey and Jordan where Syrian opposition people are located. They have to be able to get out and move around.

And I am going to be very honest with you. In the post-Benghazi atmosphere, it is much harder for professional diplomats to get out and do the kind of discussions, blunt talk, that I was just talking about, and that is going to also have to be changed.

Mr. DeSantis. The gentleman's time has expired.

Chair now recognizes the gentlemen from Illinois, Mr. Kinzinger, for 5 minutes.

Mr. Kinzinger. Thank you, Mr. Chairman.

Thank you all for being here.

When we pulled out of Iraq in 2011, did any of you all not seeing this coming? I mean, I ask that, I guess, rhetorically. I mean, I am no, like, crystal ball owner, but I knew this was going to happen. Right? I knew that if we didn't leave a residual force, this was going to fall apart.

By the way, it is a great lesson for Afghanistan as we look forward too, the importance of a residual force there.

To the folks that talk about how basically we don't want to engage in this fight, we don't get to pick the world we live in. Right? I mean, I would wish a different world if I could, I would wish a different situation if I could. But the United States can only be defeated in a case like this by our will. We are never going to be defeated militarily. I think our will was defeated in 2011 with the pullout of Iraq.

I think when with you put a red line down to say no U.S. Boots on the ground, you are in essence saying that, okay, the existence of ISIS is unacceptable unless it takes American boots to destroy ISIS, in which case American boots are worse, the existence of American boots on the ground are worse than the presence of ISIS.

So, I mean, I think we have to never put on the table what we are not willing to do. It sends a very bad message.

I just got back from Iraq about 5 or 6 weeks ago with this committee, and I have got to tell you, I went into Turkey, met with leadership of the Free Syrian Army. I was heartbroken by how they have continually been let down by the government. Promised no-fly zones of protection, promised arming and equipping, training and equipping, and over 3 years waiting for this kind of manna to come down to help them in their fight, and instead they continue to fight a two-front war against a brutal Assad.

Which, by the way, Bashar al-Assad, if I hear it again I am going to pull my hair out, is no friend of the United States, no friend to Christianity, no friend to the West. He is a brutal dictator that slaughters his own people and created an environment for ISIS to explode and exist today. Period. No Christ I follow, no Christ I look up to would call a guy like Bashar al-Assad a friend. He is a murderer and he is a brutal dictator, and he needs deposed, and hopefully peacefully, but he needs to be gone, and that needs to be the focus of the mission of the United States of America. This is going to take a long time, but if you are going to kill the incubator of ISIS, you are going to destroy the incubator of ISIS, it starts with the regime of Bashar al-Assad.

The other thing I want to say about that, so 1 year ago or so when we were debating the red line in Syria, I took my fair share of hits from people calling my office because I was very aggressive about the need to follow through on the strike in Syria. I also remember that as that discussion was happening, all over the world there were discussions about an off-ramp for Bashar al-Assad, maybe we can get him $½ billion and send him to some other country and let him live the rest of his life in peace.

After we failed to enforce the red line, there has not been one serious discussion about Bashar al-Assad being deposed from power. That is what happens when you put something on the table and you don't follow through with it.

When I went into Erbil as part of this trip, I saw the tragedy of a girl who has her two younger siblings with her, lost her parents, one of the kids is 5 years old with cerebral palsy that can't even be fed, he looks like a skeleton, because everybody was caught off guard by the intensity of this.

This is not a problem that is going to go away by us exercising restraint. I don't think we need large amounts of boots on the ground, but I think when you take them off the table, I think you just show the enemy what you are not willing to do and you encourage them.

I am encouraged by the air strikes. I think it is important to do. But, Dr. Kagan, let me ask you. How does the amount of air strikes and the intensity of air strikes we have done compare to prior engagements, for instance, the opening of Iraq in 2003?

Ms. KAGAN. The numbers of air strikes that we are conducting now do not, in my opinion as a military historian, constitute an air campaign of the size and scale that we saw, for example, at the beginning of Operation Enduring Freedom in Afghanistan. We are talking about an order, two orders of magnitude difference.

Mr. KINZINGER. Yeah. In a country the size of California, by the way, basically.

And so you think about that. I fly ISR. I still fly in the Air Guard, and I can tell you, ISR, there is all kinds of ways to acquire your target. One of them is by simply looking at it. That is what we have to rely on basically now, because we don't have assets on the ground that can target things.

So I can tell you 100 times I have looked at trucks with people in the back of them that look like fighting men, and we are not sure if they are fighting men or not. And so what happens in an air campaign like against ISIS today is they probably don't strike that target, because you don't have other verification, because the last thing you want to do is to strike a truck where it is a family going off to a family reunion.

And so, look, I am supportive of the President doing something in Iraq. He needs to step it up. I think we have to look at giving heavy weapons to the Peshmerga who are fighting our own heavy weapons that were stolen from ISIS. And we need to call this what it is. The President has got to talk to the American people about what ISIS is, the existence of them, how unacceptable it is, and how he will refuse to let them exist in the future.

With that, I thank you. I spent most of my time talking, but I yield back.

Mr. DeSantis. Gentleman yields back.

The Chair now recognizes the gentleman from Illinois, Mr. Schneider, for 5 minutes.

Mr. Schneider. Thank you, Mr. Chairman.

And, again, thank you to the witnesses.

Dr. Kagan, in your written testimony you talked about that we must raise our gaze from the tactics of fighting ISIS, and then talked about a fight that is not going to last years but run across generations. And I would like to spend my limited time here talking a little bit about that. And I think we have to look back, because what we see here is as much as anything a conflict that runs across thousands of years. You have the split between the Persians and the Arabs, the Sunni-Shi'a split. Also I think we are seeing the collapse of the borders from 1916, the Sykes-Picot borders, and the associated state structures with that in Iraq and Syria for sure, and then as you mentioned, the rise of global jihad.

In all of those, if I think through and listen to what you guys are saying, we have a number of objectives. To limit Iranian influence. To preserve—and I am saying this as a statement, but it is a question—preserve the nation-states that were created in 1916, but to do it in a way that does not include—certainly does not include Assad. To find a path within those states for pluralism that bridges the gap between the Sunnis and the Shi'as. And within all of that to defeat ISIS and global jihadism in general.

What does that strategy look like across generations as we raise our gaze? And I will open that to the entire panel.

Ms. Kagan. Thank you. It is a wonderful question.

I actually want to go back and challenge just one thing in the premise of the question, which is the notion that the kind of conflict we are seeing right now in Iraq and Syria is the kind of conflict that is thousands of years old. The point is that there are actually rather unique and special conditions in the history of these policies that is generating this tension now—a failure of states, a failure of leaders, and a deliberate radicalization of the population.

And the reason I stress that is because we can think that engaging in diminishing a regional sectarian war is impossible if we really think about it as a war that has lasted 1,000 years, but if we actually see it as a product of states' geopolitics and ideology of a moment, I think we have more room to work forward.

So what do we do? Well, the first thing I would say is we need to make sure that generations more fighters are not created right now. What we are seeing in Syria reminds me of what we saw in Afghanistan in the 1980s and 1990s. And so protraction of this conflict is not in the interest of the United States at all, because it will create not only a cadre of seasoned fighters on all sides, pro-Assad regime, pro-Iranian, pro-ISIS, pro-al-Qaeda. It will not only create those seasoned fighters and give them their combat patches so that they can fight in the future, it will actually create, as it has, refugees who are extraordinarily vulnerable to radicalization and a degree of success for global jihadis that will attract people who are vulnerable.

Mr. Schneider. I am sorry to take back time which is so limited.

Ambassador Ford, your perspective having been on the ground and spent so much time with the people throughout this territory?

Mr. FORD. Congressman, there is really one root cause of what is happening in the Islamic State and al-Nusra. Across the Levant and into Iraq there is a Sunni Arab population that feels it is under attack, feels that it has been tread upon. In Syria it has suffered probably almost 150,000 killed. In Iraq that population, which is a minority, ruled the country, but since rule was wrested away by the American forces in 2003, it feels there it has also been tread upon, treated unfairly, et cetera.

You can't fix this problem until you deal with some of those grievances, and you deal with some of those grievances by figuring out ways to have power sharing in central governments, whatever the borders are, by having large measures of decentralization, which is going to be new in that region. They have not had that before, but that is clearly what is going to be needed, it has worked with the Kurds and it will work with the Sunni Arabs in Iraq, I think. And you are going to need help from the regional states, whether that be border control so that jihadis don't slip over the border and go fight, whether that be stopping money flows from private citizens, or whether that be agreeing on a broad framework of what the states should look like in order to get to that political deal.

Mr. SCHNEIDER. Thank you. I am out of time. I yield back.

Mr. DeSANTIS. Gentleman's time has expired.

The Chair now recognizes the incoming junior Senator from the great State of Arkansas, Mr. Cotton.

Mr. COTTON. Thank you.

Dr. Kagan, how many troops did General Lloyd Austin recommend that the President retain in Iraq in 2011?

Ms. KAGAN. Mr. Cotton, I do not remember the exact number, but I have heard in media that we were talking about 10,000 to 20,000 troops.

Mr. COTTON. Okay. And the President didn't take that action. He withdrew all troops in 2011.

Ms. KAGAN. Correct.

Mr. COTTON. Based on your best understanding, whether from briefings, understanding this is an unclassified hearing, and also your professional military judgment, had the President accepted that recommendation in 2011, how many troops do you think would be in Iraq today?

Ms. KAGAN. I think that THE residual force that we had left in Iraq would be in Iraq, but I think that Iraq would be a different place in 2014 if we had, as the United States, left troops behind in 2011, because the presence of Americans at that time would have been an important check on some of the abuses of the Iraqi Government that other members have spoken of, and would be an important deterrent both to the Islamic State and to Iranian militias.

Mr. COTTON. So had we retained that residual force of reportedly 10,000 to 20,000, it would have provided a check on the Maliki government sectarianism, might have kept the Sunnis and the Kurds more tightly in the fold, contributed to the professional development of the Iraqi Army, stopped Iranian intermeddling, certainly stopped the Islamic State. Iraq would be in a better place and perhaps we would have many fewer troops there than 10,000 to 20,000 today?

Ms. KAGAN. I agree that leaving a residual force behind in early phases of turning over not the sovereignty of a government but the security of a government and its people to a nation can actually be an important way of diminishing the risks of future conflicts and the risks of having to redeploy American forces to suppress that greater level of conflict in the future.

Mr. COTTON. And with the President's latest announcement that he would authorize the deployment of another 1,500 troops to Iraq, if I have done the rough math correctly, I think we are now somewhere between 3,000 and 4,000 troops going to Iraq?

Ms. KAGAN. Correct.

Mr. COTTON. Does this seem like a slow motion tacit admission by the President that he made a mistake in 2011 in not accepting General Austin's judgment, in your opinion?

Ms. KAGAN. I do not think that the White House in general has fully recognized the error of its judgment in 2011, as a citizen observing.

Mr. COTTON. Thank you.

The title of this hearing is "Next Steps on U.S. Foreign Policy." Having reviewed the history of foreign policy, I think it is best to hear next steps, and we are of course the Congress, and we are entrusted with some important responsibilities on foreign policy, but the executive is obviously entrusted with even more. But looking ahead to the following weeks, but maybe in particular 6 or 7 weeks from now, could you give us your thoughts on what the next best steps are for us as a legislature in our system of government on Syria and Iraq, recognizing that the President under our Constitution has a somewhat free hand.

Start with Ambassador Ford to get his advice and counsel, and then maybe move down the panel for as long as we have.

Mr. FORD. Congressman, I think looking ahead, strong authorization to use military force sends the right messages to all sides. Second, reapproving the money to work with the vetted opposition in Syria, the moderate opposition. And then third, demanding accountability from the Iraqis in return for the assistance we provide. The corruption problems, the leadership problems that have been endemic, I think the Prime Minister of Iraq, Abadi, has made some changes among generals, about two dozen. It is great, frankly a little overdue, but it is good. But that won't be the end of it. There are a lot of corrupt junior officers, shall I say, or less senior. So those three things to start.

Mr. COTTON. Ambassador Abrams.

Mr. ABRAMS. I would just add it is important for the President, in the aftermath of the President's letter to the Ayatollah Khamenei, for the U.S. Government to clarify that we are not partners with Assad and that we maintain the policy that Assad must go.

Mr. COTTON. My time has expired, a constraint under which I soon will not chafe as the junior Senator from Arkansas, I suppose.

Mr. DESANTIS. Well, actually, as a parting gift, if you would like another 60 seconds to show just how appreciative I am that you won by almost 20 points in what was supposed to be a toss-up race.

Mr. COTTON. I will just let Dr. Kagan and Dr. Heydemann answer the question that I posed.

Ms. KAGAN. I agree with Ambassador Ford, and in addition I recommend that the United States show its strength in the world by ending the sequester that is limiting our ability to project force now and in the future, and that we strengthen the capabilities and authorizations for our intelligence services so that we can be prepared for this global threat.

Mr. HEYDEMANN. Thank you.

I have been particularly concerned that the current policy seems to believe that we can address the challenge of ISIS without respond to the Syria conflict and respond to the Syria conflict without addressing the challenge of ISIS. These two problems cannot be separated. There needs to be an integrated strategy that encompasses both of these concerns. And I would encourage Congress to use every possible opportunity to move the administration toward a policy framework in which the connections between the two are very explicit and built into the tactics and strategy that the White House advances.

Mr. COTTON. Thank you all.

Mr. DESANTIS. The gentleman's time has expired.

Chair now recognizes the gentleman from Rhode Island for 5 minutes.

Mr. CICILLINE. Thank you, Mr. Chairman.

And thank you to our witnesses for this important testimony. And I particularly thank you, Ambassador Ford, for your extraordinary service to our country.

I think there is no question that we all recognize the very serious threat of ISIL and the responsibility of the United States to have a coordinated strategic unified approach to this. I think this hearing is particularly important as we are about to consider a $5.6 billion request from the President to fund additional military action in Iraq and Syria, and there are many of us who have been calling for a full debate and a war authorization because Congress plays an important role in this, and I was pleased to hear everyone say that that would be useful in the context of whatis happening.

First I want to just ask you, Ambassador Ford, you have said a couple of times that as one of the three suggestions demand accountability among the Iraqi security forces. What does that look like? How would we effectively ensure accountability? Because I think everyone here would agree with that, but we are all very familiar with the pervasive corruption in the Iraqi security forces. What kinds of things, what sorts of measures would you recommend that we could press for that would bring the kind of accountability that would make them a better partner?

Mr. FORD. The reason the Iraqi Army fell apart in Mosul and the blitzkrieg went all the way down to the outskirts of Baghdad is because the Iraqi Army had bad leadership and it was corrupt. It is a lesson to us that if they don't fix this problem, no matter how much money, how much equipment we give them, it is not going to work.

So what that looks like to me is that as we send advisors in, when they identify this commander over here, that commander over there is a problem, we are not going to work with that unit at all until he is fixed, until he is changed. It may require, for example, even general flag officers who are encouraging lower level officers to say that their command staff needs salaries for 1,000 soldiers when they know perfectly well there are only 300 on duty and they are pocketing 700 soldiers' salaries for their own use, maybe that general has to go too.

But you have to be able to say to them: We can't work with you like this. And I have to be honest, I have not seen us do that very often in Iraq, frankly. Congresswoman Ros-Lehtinen was talking about what Brett McGurk, Deputy Assistant Secretary Brett McGurk had said. We knew a lot of these problems were in the Iraqi Army before. This is not a surprise to us. But I don't know that we were insisting that we can't work with them if they don't make changes.

Mr. CICILLINE. And do you, Ambassador Ford, Dr. Kagan, see any evidence that the current efforts underway both with air strikes and other efforts on the ground are having any impact on the Assad regime's kind of recalculation or reassessment? Are these efforts in any way causing the regime to contemplate a different path forward? Because everyone speaks about the necessity of some political solution, which, frankly, in the context of the facts on the ground, it is hard to imagine these power-sharing discussions and other things. So I am just wondering whether we are seeing any evidence at all that that is making a difference.

Mr. FORD. In some cases, Congressman, it has been negative difference. Let me give you an example. The Islamic State had elements of the Assad regime surrounded in a provincial capital in eastern Syria, a place called Deir ez-Zor, been under siege for months, and there was an attack lining up that would have cost the Assad regime a lot of soldiers, a lot of equipment. American air strikes forced the Islamic State to withdraw. The regime was able to reopen supply lines. And actually what the regime did was shift air aspects to go hit moderates up in northern Syria. You might remember there was reporting in the American media about how the regime intensified air operations against our friends because of the air strikes that we were doing.

So I do think that a powerful authorization to use military force will compel Assad to wonder if the Americans over time will not adjust their tactics to include his, frankly, slowly degrading air force.

Mr. CICILLINE. And could I just ask—I too won my election by 20 points—if I could have 1 more minute.

With respect to this sort of choice, and it is not necessarily a choice, but as we think about this effort to continue to train and arm the Syrian opposition versus—or in addition to—or sort of allocating resources to arming the Peshmerga, what is your assessment, Dr. Kagan, Ambassador Ford, Doctor, in terms of this likely success of this arm-and-train effort of the Syrian opposition? And if you had unlimited resources, where would you put those resources as between those two choices?

Ms. KAGAN. The effort to arm and train the Syrian moderate opposition is essential, but we, the United States, have asymmetric capabilities that we need to bring to bear on the fight in Syria in order for that moderate opposition to survive long enough to be armed and trained and make a meaningful difference on the battle-field. Namely, we do need to provide them with close air support, and we do need to reconsider targeting the Assad regime, and in particular his asymmetric capability, which comes in his use of air power against those moderates. We need to have those things together in Syria in order to create conditions for success.

Mr. HEYDEMANN. I endorse everything that Dr. Kagan said, but would add that we also need to invest adequately in creating the appropriate infrastructure to ensure that the forces that we train and equip can perform effectively and that in the areas in which they are operational we will not simply be clearing ISIS from communities that will then see the return of alternative extremist groups once that task has been accomplished.

That means building the appropriate command-and-control structures and political accountability structures led by Syrians that will ensure the effectiveness of the train-and-equip mission over time. And I am concerned that significant questions about what that infrastructure will look like have not yet been adequately answered.

Mr. CICILLINE. I thank you, Mr. Chairman, for the indulgence. Thank you. Yield back.

Mr. DESANTIS. Gentleman's time has expired.

Just real quickly, Ambassador Ford, you had mentioned that an authorization of force would send a message to Iran. A lot of us are concerned about these nuclear negotiations. The President has said—well, it has been reported—that they don't want to even go through Congress. They want to keep it away from Congress, which tells me that it may not be a deal that would merit approval from Congress or the American people. And so I am certainly losing patience with that.

Do you think a vote against a bad nuclear deal or a vote to reimpose tough sanctions would also be a good signal to send to Iran vis-à-vis our fight in Syria and Iraq?

Mr. FORD. The most important thing, Congressman, with respect to Iraq and to Syria is to get the Iranians to adjust their behavior. They can't just use Shi'a militia to fix the Islamic State problem on the eastern front in Iraq. The Shi'a militia will drive the Sunni Arabs right into the hands further of the Islamic State. And in Syria, the Iranians have got to accept that Bashar is going to go and there is going to be some other kind of a government.

So I don't know how the nuclear negotiations are going to directly affect that, but what I do think is that we need to find a way to get the Iranians to understand that there may be other ways to fix the Islamic State problem without doing it the way they are doing it, which is actually making the problem infinitely worse.

To be frank, Assad and the Iranians are helping create the Islamic State problem. I talked about this aggrieved Sunni community. The Iranians are the biggest single problem behind that.

Mr. DESANTIS. No, absolutely. And, look, just from my time, I was in the Al Anbar province, and the more Iran is involved, I mean, that is a total repellant. I mean, they would much prefer ISIS than an Iranian-backed government. And so it would make the whole enterprise, I think, go up in smoke.

Mr. FORD. You understand because you were in Anbar. This is the accountability aspect that I am talking about.

Mr. DESANTIS. Absolutely.

Well, I just wanted to thank the witnesses. We really appreciated your testimony, taking the time here to answer our questions. I think all your thoughts were very considered and I know it will help the committee members very much.

And so with that, this hearing stands adjourned.

[Whereupon, at 5 o'clock p.m., the subcommittee was adjourned.]

APPENDIX

MATERIAL SUBMITTED FOR THE RECORD

SUBCOMMITTEE HEARING NOTICE
COMMITTEE ON FOREIGN AFFAIRS
U.S. HOUSE OF REPRESENTATIVES
WASHINGTON, DC 20515-6128

Subcommittee on the Middle East and North Africa
Ileana Ros-Lehtinen (R-FL), Chairman

November 13, 2014

TO: MEMBERS OF THE COMMITTEE ON FOREIGN AFFAIRS

You are respectfully requested to attend an OPEN hearing of the Committee on Foreign Affairs, to be held by the Subcommittee on the Middle East and North Africa in Room 2172 of the Rayburn House Office Building (and available live on the Committee website at www.foreignaffairs.house.gov):

DATE: Wednesday, November 19, 2014

TIME: 2:30 p.m.

SUBJECT: Next Steps for U.S. Foreign Policy on Syria and Iraq

WITNESSES: The Honorable Robert Stephen Ford
                   Senior Fellow
                   Middle East Institute
                   (Former U.S. Ambassador to Syria)

                   The Honorable Elliott Abrams
                   Senior Fellow for Middle Eastern Studies
                   Council on Foreign Relations

                   Kimberly Kagan, Ph.D.
                   Founder and President
                   Institute for the Study of War

                   Steven Heydemann, Ph.D.
                   Vice President of Applied Research on Conflict
                   United States Institute of Peace

By Direction of the Chairman

The Committee on Foreign Affairs seeks to make its facilities accessible to persons with disabilities. If you are in need of special accommodations, please call 202/225-5021 at least four business days in advance of the event, whenever practicable. Questions with regard to special accommodations in general (including availability of Committee materials in alternative formats and assistive listening devices) may be directed to the Committee.

COMMITTEE ON FOREIGN AFFAIRS

MINUTES OF SUBCOMMITTEE ON _____ *Middle East and North Africa* _____ HEARING

Day___*Wednesday*___Date___*19 November 2014*___Room_____*2172*_____

Starting Time ___*3:25 PM*___ Ending Time ___*5:00 PM*___

Recesses |__*0*__| (____to ____)(____to ____)(____to ____)(____to ____)(____to ____)(____to ____)

Presiding Member(s)

Chairman Ros-Lehtinen; Rep. DeSantis

Check all of the following that apply:

Open Session ☑︎   Electronically Recorded (taped) ☑︎
Executive (closed) Session ☐   Stenographic Record ☑︎
Televised ☑︎

TITLE OF HEARING:

Next Steps for U.S. Foreign Policy on Syria and Iraq

SUBCOMMITTEE MEMBERS PRESENT:

Chairman Ros-Lehtinen, Raking Member Deutch, Reps. Chabot, Cicilline, Cotton, DeSantis, Higgins, Kennedy, Kinzinger, Schneider, Yoho,

NON-SUBCOMMITTEE MEMBERS PRESENT: *(Mark with an * if they are not members of full committee.)*

None

HEARING WITNESSES: Same as meeting notice attached? Yes ☑︎ No ☐
(If "no", please list below and include title, agency, department, or organization.)

STATEMENTS FOR THE RECORD: *(List any statements submitted for the record.)*

SFR - Rep. Connolly

TIME SCHEDULED TO RECONVENE _____
or
TIME ADJOURNED ___*5:00 PM*___

Subcommittee Staff Director

Statement for the Record
Submitted by Mr. Connolly of Virginia

Without clearly defined long-term goals in Syria and Iraq, we will be consumed by the hourly emerging threats that have set the region on fire and demanded a robust military response from the U.S. and our international partners. In Syria, Bashar al-Assad's brutal regime has committed systematic atrocities against his own civilians. The domestic conflict he has fomented has developed into a breeding ground for violent terrorist groups, including the Islamic State of Syria and the Levant (ISIL). The President has already stated that Assad lacks legitimacy, and I cannot imagine a long-term U.S. strategy in Syria that does not seek to find a viable alternative to Assad. However, it is not enough to eradicate threats to America's national security and regional stability. Our actions today must sow the seeds for a better tomorrow in Syria and Iraq. The U.S. should first put itself on firm legal footing by carrying out military strikes under a new Authorization for the Use of Military Force (AUMF). The U.S. also must continue to build on our international coalition and bolster reliable partners on the ground in Syria and Iraq. Failure to do so would place an unsustainable burden on U.S. resources and troops and leave the region ill-equipped to function without a ubiquitous U.S. presence in-perpetuity.

This Committee laid bare for the world to see the barbaric and inhumane manner in which Bashar al-Assad has treated political opposition and dissent in Syria. At the Full Committee hearing on July 31, our guest witness, "Caesar," testified that he defected from the Syrian military with over 50,000 photos of Syrians who were tortured and murdered by the Assad regime. The proof for his story was his collection of meticulously catalogued photos and records that documented the scale and brutality of the regime's genocidal operation. Caesar's photos confirmed what many members of the Committee had already concluded when we passed by unanimous vote, H. Con. Res. 51, a measure directing the U.S. representative to the United Nations to promote the establishment of a Syrian war crimes tribunal.

In addition to the 10,000 suspected victims of torture and extrajudicial killings, 200,000 Syrians have died during the country's bloody civil war. Nearly 10 million refugees have been displaced because of the fighting with more than 3 million seeking shelter in and straining the resources of neighboring countries. The fighting has touched every corner of Syria. Terrorists groups have used the ensuing chaos to expand their numbers and sources of revenue and make territorial gains. Though Iraq is where ISIL originated, it was in the fire of the Syrian civil war that its newfound organizational strength was forged.

Fighting that emanated from the civil war has spilled across the Syrian border into neighboring Iraq. Hard-fought gains after a decade of war in Iraq have been reversed. Nowhere is this more clearly demonstrated than in the city of Fallujah, the site of site of building-to-building combat in 2004 that resulted in more than 100 American soldiers killed in action and over 1,000 casualties. ISIL took control of Fallujah in January 2014 during its sweep across western Iraq and maintains control to this day.

ISIL was able to exploit dissatisfaction with the Nouri al-Maliki Administration which was found to have provoked sectarian strife and weakened the Iraqi Security Forces (ISF) with sectarian-based purges. Fortunately, the U.S. concluded that Maliki was not a viable partner going forward and supported the formation of a new government. It is now up to the administration of Haider al-Abadi to prove that it values the stability of Iraq and the safety of its people over the cynical consolidation of power. Reports of a spring-time offensive led by 20,000 Iraqi troops are an encouraging sign of ownership and initiative on the part of the Iraqi government. The Haider Administration could broadcast further resolve by supporting and coordinating with the Peshmerga forces of Iraqi Kurdistan. The Peshmerga have demonstrated competency and determination on the battlefield in the face of the ISIL threat. U.S. policy should recognize that support for the Peshmerga is essential to repelling ISIL. The manner in which we provide assistance to these forces should be further evaluated if the government in Baghdad proves incapable of coordination with the Peshmerga and supporting their shared fight.

The Syrian crisis is also impacting NATO ally Turkey and major non-NATO ally Jordan. Both countries have absorbed over 1 million Syrian refugees and heavy fighting persists along their borders with Syria. It is incumbent upon the U.S., as part of our foreign policy in Iraq and Syria, to ensure that we coordinate with vital regional allies and support decisive action to mitigate the threats posed by ISIL and the Syrian civil war. The legislation offered by Chairman Ros-Lehtinen, H. R. 5648, to improve defense cooperation between the United States and the Hashemite Kingdom of Jordan, deserves further discussion, and hopefully it can be a constructive measure on this front.

Despite receiving authorization from the Turkish parliament to launch military actions into Iraq and Syria, Turkish President Recep Tayyip Erdoğan has preconditioned Turkey's full cooperation in Syria with demands for "safe zones" and a more comprehensive strategy to topple Bashar al-Assad. The U.S. must work to create a united front, and one could envision an active role for Turkey as part of the broad international coalition working to create the kind of stability that would seriously undermine the grip ISIL and Assad have on the region.

In September, the House of Representatives passed an amendment to H. J. Res. 124, the continuing resolution, to authorize the President to train and equip appropriately vetted Syrian opposition forces. I appreciated that the measure addressed many concerns that were initially raised about the effort. First, the amendment provided for careful Congressional oversight. The Department of Defense must report to Congress on the vetting process for trainees 15 days prior to providing any such assistance. The President must report to Congress on how this operation fits within our overall regional strategy. The Department of Defense must also submit a report every 90 days updating Congress on the status of the operation. These are prudent measures and consistent with the Constitutional role of Congressional oversight. Second, the amendment did not provide a blank check for military operations. No additional funds are provided by the measure, and the Department of Defense must submit reprogramming requests to Congress. Third, it did not allow for an open-ended commitment. The limited activities authorized by the amendment will remain in effect until the earlier of the date of the expiration of the CR or the enactment of the FY2015 National Defense Authorization Act.

However, a major complication that arises from the effort to equip and train the Syrian opposition is the difficulty of identifying reliable Syrian opposition forces. The opposition forces are not wearing white hats and black hats and their allegiances are sometimes fluid as evidenced by reports earlier this month of Free Syrian Army rebels surrendering, and some even defecting, to al-Qaeda linked al-Nusra fighters. The Congressional oversight provisions included in the H. J. Res. 124 will be essential to evaluating our ability to discern friend from foe.

The amendment to H. J. Res. 124 was never meant to grant Congressional authorization for the use of direct military force to combat the growing threat posed by ISIL to America and our allies. Quite the contrary, the amendment specifically prohibited the introduction of U.S. Armed Forces into hostilities.

Instead, the President has authorized military strikes in Iraq and Syria under the 2001 AUMF against those who perpetrated the terrorist attacks of 9/11 and associated forces. The President has said that he welcomes Congressional support for his effort to show the world we are "united in confronting this danger." However, I would suggest that the 2001 AUMF has gone stale, and that the President needs specific Congressional authority for a prolonged campaign in Iraq and Syria.

While this issue has been the subject of a long-simmering debate between our branches of government and among historians and scholars, I would note that the Constitution grants only Congress the power to declare war. Anything short of debating a new AUMF would be an abrogation of our sworn duty to defend and support the Constitution. I was deeply dismayed when this Congress went into recess for 7 weeks instead of asserting our Constitutional authority and debating a matter of war and peace, and I am troubled by the reports suggesting a compromise in next year's defense authorization bill will leave this matter unresolved.

We must assert Congressional prerogative to make crystal clear to the administration, our allies, our constituents, and even our military families the circumstances and parameters under which we would once again authorize engagement by our men and women in uniform in this tumultuous region of the world. House Concurrent Resolution 105, which we adopted in July, prohibits the President from deploying or maintaining U.S. armed forces in a sustained combat role in Iraq without specific statutory authorization. That resolution correctly reinforced the role Congress must play in this debate, and now that the President has developed a bold and decisive strategy to thwart and turn back ISIL, it is time for us take the next step and authorize the specific actions that will be taken to achieve it.

It is only within full view of the law that we can lead a comprehensive international response to the crises in Iraq and Syria while remaining a committed partner and beacon of democracy to allies and those on the ground that would rely upon our assistance and model their society upon our example.

www.ingramcontent.com/pod-product-compliance
Lightning Source LLC
Chambersburg PA
CBHW080544290526
45790CB00006B/2542